Cultivating Compassion

Creating Self

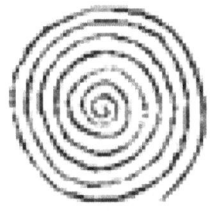

Dr. Terri L. Russ

WWW.TEHOMCENTER.ORG

Cultivating Compassion Creating Self
ISBN: Softcover 978-1-960326-48-5

Tehom Center Publishing is an imprint publishing feminist and queer authors, with a commitment to elevating BIPOC writers. Amplifying authors from the margins bent on writing toward justice is our calling and joy.

In addition to traditional, independent publishing at no cost to the author, Tehom Center Publishing also offers one-on-one and group coaching that empowers authors in book writing, book marketing, and book entrepreneurship through an intersectionally feminist lens.

Learn more at www.tehomcenter.org/tehom-center-publishing

Cultivating Compassion

Creating Self

Dedication

To Blue, Lulu, and Bowen with a wish they continue to embrace their creativity.

Contents

Acknowledgements

Creating a book, especially a book filled with personal reminisces and asides, is a momentous task. Even though the author gets most of the credit, the work doesn't happen without a lot of other people helping out. Taking the time to acknowledge and thank those people is an equally momentous task and one filled with the possibility of missing someone. With that in mind, I will attempt this task and will ask for forgiveness should I overlook anyone in the process.

I wouldn't have made it to this point without the unwavering encouragement and love of Regina. Her patience in listening to me muse on the myriad words wrangling in my head and her gentle nudging to keep me moving forward were pivotal in helping me get out of my own way. My ride or die, Jen, has been with me through many of my creative and professional life changes and continues to respond to even my most random texts with humor, encouragement, support, and inspiration. Shelly, Marne, Chip, Nell, and Lisa all provided unwavering friendship, thoughtful feedback, and inspiring encouragement along the way that enriched every word in these pages. All of your contributions have illuminated and continue to inspire my path of embracing my creativity. I am deeply grateful to have all of you in my life. A special thanks to McKenzie for helping me with all the behind-scenes tech stuff that I need as much as I dread it and for always asking the question that helps me level up my creative ambitions. A heartfelt thanks to all of the students I have had the privilege to teach over the years and to those who have continued as friends for helping me find new and creative ways to teach and inspire. To all of the individuals whose stories help bring my words to life, I thank you for being a part of my journey.

Angela, thank you for responding to that initial query and for continuing to believe in me and this project. I know that my thoughts and words have been transformed into something better than I ever imagined with your insights and assistance. I look forward to all the next projects we will work on together.

Ginny, Blue, Lulu, and Bowen thank you for continuing the creative journey. I know that all of you will continue to grow ever more awesome with each year.

I Wanted to Be a Renaissance Man

I don't remember how old I was when I decided I wanted to be a Renaissance man. I'm sure it was one of the many times I was grounded for being too much, always too much, and in lieu of being able to play outside I was spending lots of time hanging out in the library.[1] Libraries and books always were my refuge, my safe place, and even today, when I find myself overworked and overstressed I take comfort in getting lost in a book. I was privileged to grow up before the time of overscheduling kids' lives became the norm, so I was able to spend hours alone combing through the library shelves. Since I found myself being grounded and subject to its limitations quite frequently, my library combing time was also quite frequent.

My infatuation with being a Renaissance man came about the summer I discovered Leonard DaVinci and Michelangelo.[2] I'm sure that during my combing of the shelves, I had gotten bored with the children's section and wandered into the adult stacks looking for something new and interesting to read. I must have found a book or books explaining their lives and their works. The name of the book is long forgotten, but the glorious expansiveness of its discovery and secrets lingers. Renaissance Men did everything. They painted. They wrote. They designed. They were masters of many things. I grew up under the shadow of the threat of being a jack of all trades and master of none; yet here were these two men defying that dictate. I was especially fascinated by the fact that one of them, DaVinci, only

---

[1] I was a pretty precocious kid so I think being able to go to the library also provided my mom with some much needed respite from me.

[2] I don't really know if it was summer when I found them but in the retelling of the memory over the years, it always feels like it was summer so that has become the narrative.

slept 20 minutes every four hours.[3] The most interesting aspect of them, however, was the fact they did a lot and did it all well. This ideal of the Renaissance Man as a jack of all trades and master of all trades was what I aspired to be.

I started telling anyone who would listen that I was setting out on my journey to be a Renaissance Man. Long before the days of open discussions on gender fluidity, the more sarcastic in my audience would say something along the lines of, "But you're not a man, and why would you want to be like that anyway?" The more tactful would say things such as, "I remember when I was a child. I wish I could return to those days of not having to worry about reality"; or "Enjoy it while you can and before you have to grow up and be responsible for bills and a family and everything." Harsh? It's hard not to consider these words harsh. We were a working class family surrounded by other working class families, and while it never really felt like we were poor, as an adult reflecting on that time I can see how we struggled and didn't have as much as many others.[4] In the context of that environment, those harsh words are actually caring words delivering the reality of working class life where survival often depends upon hard work and long hours.

Perhaps the larger and more damaging message I received from my foray into wanting to be a Renaissance man, though, was that "real adults" held "real jobs." They worked to make a living and a life for themselves and their families. The work of working was serious and strenuous and left little room for frittering away time in creative activities. Implied within this message was that it was ok to be creative as a hobby, but what really counted was hard work as defined by your job. I internalized this message in ways that I may not ever fully understand. As I passed into my teen and early adult

---

[3] I have yet to master this feat, mostly because I like sleeping, but maybe one day.
[4] This point became especially clear when I looked up my childhood home on Zillow and realized it was less than 1000 square feet.

years, my dreams of being a Renaissance man faded into the background as I began working hard at working. I worked a few different jobs – waitressing, delivering pizzas, bartending, running an antique store, making copies in a hospital copy shop, teaching aerobics, and for a flitting moment of early entrepreneurship, I sold Tupperware.[5] Eventually, I earned a few college degrees and over the years settled into the life of being a professor. I spent my days teaching or planning to teach. I conducted rigorous research and wrote about my findings. I served on campus committees and gave back to my local community through activism and board service. I kept a good balance between work and my hobbies, or so I thought.

Life was good, and I probably wouldn't have ever thought otherwise if it weren't for COVID and lockdown.[6] When we first went into lockdown, I was kind of excited. As an introvert, I looked forward to being able to stay home and not have to make excuses for why I didn't want to go out. In those early days, like so many other people, I figured we would be dealing with this COVID mess for a couple of weeks before life would return to normal. I quickly settled into a daily lockdown routine. Every morning I would get up and start the coffee making process while letting the Diva Dog out. I would read the paper while drinking my first cup of coffee and then change into "real" clothes the same as I would on a normal workday. To keep myself focused on finishing my work[7], once dressed I would create a detailed list of tasks I needed to accomplish that day. These lists would be filled with school obligations, household chores, and exercise goals. A few years earlier I had started a mindfulness journey

---

[5] I could probably write an entire memoir simply on the random jobs I held before I was 30 years old.

[6] Although to be fair, I had been feeling frustrated with my profession for a few years and had been dreaming of all sorts of what ifs that might happen if I took the leap to quit.

[7] Although realistically, the work of a professor is never finished. There is always one more article to read or one more tweak to make on your class prep or several more e-mails to be answered.

and had spent a year doing yoga every day. I decided lock down was a good time to expand my mindfulness practices into daily meditations, and being the ever diligent list maker, I started adding meditation sessions to my task lists.

As the days in lockdown added up, it became apparent that this COVID thing wasn't like the flu or other viruses and that lockdown would likely be lasting more than a couple weeks. I decided to put the time to good use and learn a new skill, something fun that I wouldn't normally be able to fit into my busy schedule. I explored many options and for a short while was convinced that I would teach myself how to play mandolin, even though I didn't own a mandolin. I knew I could order one online, but after going down one too many rabbit holes trying to figure out what makes one mandolin different from another, I abandoned that thought. Around the same time, a flyer for an art sale by some online retailer crossed my radar. On a whim I decided to order paint supplies, telling myself that I always wanted to paint. Without much thought, and no research, I decided to order a watercolors kit. I didn't think much beyond the fact that it seemed like watercolors should be easier and the supplies were more quickly accessible than acrylics or oils.

Ever the good student, once I placed my order, I started researching how to paint with watercolors. Despite my love of lists, for some reason I didn't record any of this research so I'm not sure how many articles I read and videos I watched. I realized pretty quickly, however, that watercolor painting wasn't quite as easy as I imagined. Never one to back down from a challenge I kept watching and reading while waiting eagerly for my supplies. When they eventually arrived, I set up a small watercolor painting station on the front porch and started exploring. From the first brushstroke, I enjoyed it; in fact I loved the process and everything about painting. Even though I struggled with trying to control the paint to water ratios, I found my time playing with them to be relaxing and meditative.

However, always on my mind were those early, formative lessons about the importance of work. My time painting and figuring out the ratios always came after my "real" work for the day was complete.

The other thing I decided to do during lock down was spend some time deep diving into myself and reflecting on who I was as a person and how I wanted to be in the world. I have always been a reflective individual and have written hundreds of pages of journal entries over the years. In addition, when I started my journey into mindfulness I deepened my practice of self-reflection, so I felt like I was a pretty aware person. I regularly expressed gratitude in both large and small ways. I practiced being present to my life every day while also allowing myself to be human and acknowledge that mistakes happen. I also knew, however, that it is always possible to do more work and become even better. In addition, I had been growing increasingly frustrated with the demands and politics of being a professor. I knew the time for me to change professions was here, but I wasn't sure exactly what that change should look like. When a self-guided month long reflection and meditation seminar came onto my radar I jumped at the opportunity.

Once again, my good student side emerged as I dedicated another new journal[8] to this endeavor. I started the class knowing that I was going to do this well and get the most out of it as possible. Each day's lesson focused on a specific topic and presented short readings, a video, and a series of questions and activities. As I started working through the days, I felt pretty good about myself as I had already incorporated many of the suggested practices into my daily life. I became convinced that this seminar would be a way to review my mindfulness practices and maybe find one or two additional things I could add into the rotation. I was thoroughly convinced that there was nothing significant that I would take away from the 30 days and

---

[8] I love journals and finding reasons to start new ones.

decided to enjoy the time for what it was and not worry about the extra focus on me.

Not surprisingly, my hubris became my downfall[9] when on day 23 of the class, the theme for the day was creativity. I had been looking forward to this day from the beginning. The course materials laid out the outline of the entire course up front so you could see what each day's topic was. However, you couldn't access each day's material until you had completed the day before. It's interesting how once again, creativity in my life was being put on hold until the other work was done. The day of creativity finally happened, and after completing my school tasks and dutifully checking them off my list I sat down to complete my seminar task. I was expecting an exploration of what it means to be creative and perhaps some examples of ways to incorporate more creativity into my life. In my assuming I know everything way, I figured I would get in some extra painting time that day. The question for the day was: What would your life look like if you embraced your creativity? Immediately I realized how much of myself I was missing by constantly suppressing my creativity behind my "real" work. The more I reflected and mediated on the question, the more I came to understand that it felt like I was only half living and always longing for something more. My childhood goals of being a Renaissance Man resurfaced. This time, instead of embracing the reality of those harsh words from my childhood, I dared to ask myself, "What if?" What if I embraced my creativity? What if I paid as much attention to it as to my "real" work? What if my creativity is my real work?[10]

The nascent spark of an idea planted that day continued to grow, eventually overtaking my work as a professor. I now have multiple painting and studio spaces in my house and create on a daily basis.

---

[9] I say downfall but in reality it was the exact thing I didn't know I needed.
[10] This last question, when it appeared, scared me. To answer it truthfully meant to admit the depth of unhappiness I was experiencing in my professional life.

As I write this, I am in the midst of leaving my tenured position as a professor and launching my own business.[11] I hope to help others find ways to practice self-compassion in creative ways by embracing an intentional, firm commitment to practicing kindness to their individual selves as a way of then expressing compassion to others. Even though I have what looks like a thriving career and a successful life, I spend a lot of time questioning myself and getting in my own way. Throughout these meditations I reflect on my process of learning to embrace my creative side by living into my authentic self.

I didn't plan on writing these meditations. I thought I would write a book about my year of pandemic painting. I had a rough outline of that book and, ever the good academic had started researching what the "experts" had to say on creativity. To jumpstart that writing process, I decided to join the NaNoWriMo 30-day challenge in November, 2022. I decided that for 30 days I would sit down, reflect on my life, and write whatever emerged. I had no plan other than to be my most authentic self and let whatever thoughts, stories, and emotions emerged live on the page. I thought I would probably write what would be the introduction to that book. I would talk about my experiences with taking up painting and grappling with the shift in my way of being that embracing my creativity entailed, and in part that is what I wrote. I realized early on, however, that the book I thought I was going to write wasn't the book that wanted to emerge. I abandoned the concept of my year of pandemic painting and instead lived into the memories and words that demanded to be set free. I committed to being honest and authentic, sharing the proverbial good, bad, and ugly.

When I returned to my writings to start editing, I was surprised to see how many times and in how many ways, I focused on my fears.

---

[11] I initially resisted writing that sentence, and wrote it and delete it several times. I still feel a bit of angst putting that commitment into writing.

My fears of allowing myself to live into my creativity, my fears of daring to dream what being a Creative could look like, and my fears of accepting that this change was not only one that I wanted but one that needed to happen. Woven throughout is the story of my recognizing that being creative and a Creative also entails me walking away from being a tenured professor, a profession that has defined who I am for over 20 years. For me, living into my reality as a Creative is more than simply a shift in job titles; it is a shift in my entire way of being in and walking throughout the world. To embody this shift, I have to practice what I preach by being compassionate with myself. At times this is easy, at others it is difficult, seeming impossible. Sometimes I succeed, and sometimes I fail. The story I tell in here moves forward recursively -- at times it will move forward and then shift to fold back over on itself, revisiting issues already discussed. The story continues to move forward, but like life it is sometimes messy and far from a linear progression. Throughout, I share part of my journey and struggles with stepping away from who I have been and stepping into who I am meant to be – even though at this moment I still don't fully know who she is. While I don't have all the answers or even claim to have them, I hope that reading about my struggles and epiphanies helps inspire others to embrace their creative spark and find their inner Renaissance Man.

There is no one specific way to read and work with these meditations. The suggestions I present in here are merely that – suggestions. They are not mandates or rules dictating how you must work with the material. I encourage you to find a process that works best for you, even if that means completely disregarding what I suggest. Have fun and be creative!

Even if you don't consider yourself a writer, I suggest you dedicate a journal to these meditations to help you keep your thoughts in a central location and to provide a log or record of your journey. While there are many online journal options available, I suggest going the old school route of paper and pen, specifically a journal with unlined pages and pens in lots of colors.[12] The physical process of writing changes the way we interact and think about the material we are working with. The organic process of writing, instead of typing, changes the way we cognitively process our thoughts with the added bonus that we more readily remember the things we write. Another advantage to writing over typing is that we aren't interrupted by those little red and blue squiggly lines that indicate when we have spelled a word wrong or misused grammar. By changing our approach to the act of writing, we change the way we interact with our thoughts and words.

When you approach each meditation, try to begin with a clear and open mind. If you find yourself distracted with all of the tasks you "should" be doing, take a moment to write them in a list.[13] Put the list aside and know it will still be there when you are finished. Close your eyes and take a few deep cleansing breaths to help bring you into the moment. On days that I feel especially tense or stressed, I like to loudly exhale as a way to release those feelings. When you find yourself tuned into the moment, pull out your journal and pen and open the book to the meditation of the day.

Read the meditation title and question. Before reading any further, in your journal make note of any images, words, ideas, etc. that come to mind. Don't worry if the things that pop up seem odd or off or weird. Sometimes our intuition knows things or makes connections that aren't immediately clear in our conscious mind. If you create a record of these things, you can always return to it later. Remember, this is your journey and your journal. You never have to show it to anyone else unless you choose to do so. Allow yourself as much time as needed for this process before turning to read the full meditation.

_____

[12] One of my many mantras is use all the colors.
[13] Lists are an amazing gift.

As you read through the meditation then, continue this process of making note of your thoughts. When you complete the reading, allow yourself a moment to pause and breathe. Return to the opening question and reflect on it again.

I like to use an unstructured free write process when I work with reflection prompts like the ones you'll find here. After I read the prompt, I set a timer for 20 minutes and begin writing. I write everything that comes to mind without worrying about spelling or grammar.[14] Keep your pen moving the entire time. If you don't know what to write, you can simply write "I don't know what to write." Even though it may seem silly, by doing this, you begin to get out of your own way and will find yourself eventually writing things you didn't realize you were thinking about. At times you may find that when your time is up, you still have words that want to come onto the page. Keep going as long as you would like. When you do find yourself at the end of your words, close your journal and take a few deep breaths. Resist the urge to read what you just wrote as the words will still be there when you return. If you allow yourself space between the moment of writing and moment of reading, you will find that you engage with your writing differently. Often when I finish a writing jag, I am convinced that everything I wrote is horrible and will need to be deleted. More often than not, however, when I return to the words I find they are better than I remembered.

You can follow this same meditation process with painting. Use the canvas or your art journal to host the thoughts that arise. Use colors that speak to you even if they don't make sense or vary from your usual palette. Sling paint at the surface freely without worrying about what it looks like. If you don't know what to create, paint circles or dots to help focus your thoughts. Use this time to expand out of

---

[14] I lovingly think of this process as word vomit in which I vomit out everything and then come back later to clean it up.

your usual ways of creating. When you hear that voice in your head questioning your choices, and let's be honest, you know this will happen at least once, pause. Take a deep breath and remind yourself this is your journey and that you get to define how it unfolds however you wish. Keep pushing forward.

If you are feeling especially expansive, I encourage you to do both a writing journal and an art journal or canvas. Let the two processes feed into and off of each other. Break the rules and write on your canvas and paint in your writing journal. Have fun and embrace the freedom of not being accountable to anyone or for anything. Through it all, remember to breathe and be gentle with yourself. Compassion for others begins with compassion for yourself. At the end of each reflection process, it's important to acknowledge yourself for the work and dedication you have given yourself. When I teach this process, I call it Compassionate Creativity. I end each session with a peace greeting to help us close the moment and re-enter our regular lives. I have included the greeting at the end of this section, and you are welcome to use it should you choose.

Have fun and breathe deep.

May you walk in peace;

May you find peace;

May you create peace;

May you be in peace.

Meditation 1
Embrace Your Creativity

What would your life look like if you embraced your creativity?

It's always the easy questions that get me, so the more I pondered the question of what my life would look like if I embraced my creativity, the more memories overwhelmed me.

As a child I loved spending hours creating worlds. I would design complex projects and then pull out my paper and crayons to create them. I planned elaborate gifts for family that put my creative juices to good use, such as the time I decided to create a manuscript-like picture of the Lord's Prayer for my grandma. I found all the different versions of the Bible we had in the house and compared the language in each to find the best version of the prayer. I then pulled out my 64 box of crayons to print out the words. I finished it off with drawings of flowers and greenery like those I imagined would be found in ancient manuscripts. I can still picture it hanging in a frame on my grandma's bedroom wall. When I still played piano I would create musical gifts. The year that Debby Boone's "You Light Up My Life" was topping the charts, I decided to teach myself how to play it as a gift for my mother.[15] I also loved writing stories and poems about the ordinary minutiae of daily life. I would create dialogue for the spices in the cabinet or design debates between various pieces of furniture. I didn't realize it then, but I was

---

[15] I still cringe when I think about this and can only imagine what it actually sounded like. I love that version of myself who bravely dived into the process with no fear of the outcome.

practicing what would become one of my life passions – finding the extraordinary in the ordinary.

Even though I enjoyed diving into creative projects and endeavors, always lurking in the background were those messages that work, hard work, paying work, was the ultimate factor that determined your value and your success. When adults would ask what I wanted to be when I grew up and I would respond with "artist" or "writer" their responses didn't actively discourage me. Although they definitely didn't encourage me either. Instead they would say things like, "I remember when I could be so innocent and naïve", or they would look at my parents and remark, "be prepared to support this one forever. You better hope she marries rich."[16] Through repetition, these messages sunk in, becoming pals with my creative DNA.

The message, while never spoken directly to me, was clear – being creative was something that only a lucky few possessed and being a Creative was not an acceptable vocational pursuit. In other words, having creative pursuits are acceptable as long as they are kept in their proper place. I remember having an alternate version of this conversation in college with my fellow English majors. We would debate for hours over how much writing we had to do before we could consider ourselves Writers. Was it volume? Was it quality? Was it number of publications? Even though my friends and I worked as writing tutors in the college writing center and served as editors for the undergraduate literary journal, none of us dared claim the title of Writer. Even a few years after graduation when my friend and I started running open mic nights for a local coffee shop and were regular contributors of our own poetry and essays, we didn't claim the title.

---

[16] I'll save for another time, preferably with many adult beverages present, the many levels of heterosexist, patriarchal wrong in those statements.

I also started getting messages that perhaps creativity wasn't the best thing after all. While I'm sure there were many things that happened, two incidents in particular stand out. In third or fourth grade, our homework assignment was to share with the class our favorite color. I wish I could remember the purpose or goal of the assignment; perhaps I never knew. I dutifully went home and started sorting through my 64 box. I looked for any excuse to touch and organize my crayons and pencils and papers.[17] I loved colors in general but decided to focus on the assignment and limit my choice to one. I'm sure I created some sort of elaborate system of elimination but the ultimate winner was periwinkle. It continues to be a favorite of mine with how blue and violet blend to create a color that can change simply by tilting your head or shifting the light. Equally important, however, was the name – periwinkle. It's one of those words that makes your mouth happy. Say it and see if you don't smile.[18] When I took my choice to class the next day, I was shocked at the teacher's response. She rejected it as not being a "real" color. What does that even mean? Who gets to decide what is and isn't a real color? If Crayola decided it was real enough to be in the 64 box shouldn't that count? I can still feel my red cheeks of humiliation as my classmates laughed at my choice. Forced to choose something different on the spot, I opted for yellow.[19]

The second incident occurred a few years later in middle school during art class. We had art a few times a week, and I was chosen to be in the honors' section. This was important because we got to explore different styles of art as well as being allowed to use the better art supplies.[20] The assignment in question was to bring in a

---

[17] I can get lost in hours' worth of organizing art supplies.
[18] Live dangerously and say it out loud, right now. Just once, say it. C'mon you can do it.
[19] This is probably why yellows and images of suns and sunflowers appear so frequently in my paintings.
[20] I am fully aware of the inequity of this set up and will happily share that rant with anyone who wants to hear it.

greeting card picture that we liked so that we could recreate it as a painting. I chose a winter scene that featured a barn red covered bridge surrounded by snow with bits of blue water peeking through and clusters of pine trees in the background. My friend Roz and I shared our table and supplies and lots of gossip while working on our paintings. On the second day of the project our table was up for evaluation and critique by the teacher. The purpose of these critiques was to help us better understand composition and enhance our technique. My teacher remarked that I was making good progress and that my technique had a childlike feel to it. As soon as she said it, I heard Roz laugh. While I'm sure the teacher meant her comment to be a compliment on my aesthetic, that is not what I heard as an insecure middle schooler. The last thing a child who is in the throes of physical development and hormonal changes wants to be called is a child. Childlike painting, therefore, is anathema. Like any good yet insecure middle schooler would do, I brushed off her comment, shared a laugh with Roz, and pretended like I was above it all. I never did finish the painting, though.

Despite my internalization of and belief in these limiting messages, throughout my life I've always had some sort of creative side. I have always had creative hobbies, with "hobbies" being the key word. My "creativity" was something I did to relieve stress and celebrate the completion of a task or a big project. It was a past time, something I did, not part of who I was. Except, of course, that being creative is also about being a Creative. Creativity is written into my DNA. I believe it's written into everyone's DNA but that we are actively discouraged or persuaded against embracing it.

Writing in various forms has always been present in my life, but there were other pursuits as well. At various points I've become obsessed with crochet, making hats and scarves galore. For a couple years I was dedicated to creating crochet motifs in various sizes and forms, including one year where I did a 30-day motif a day challenge.[21] I became an expert at cross stitch and embroidery, creating pillows and wall hangings and even a few stuffed toys. During grad school I lived on campus in grad housing for a bit and one day stumbled into a store that sold beads and jewelry making supplies. I asked the clerk how to make earrings and quickly became obsessed with making earrings and necklaces and bracelets for everyone. The extra stress of grad school was reflected in the increasing complexity of my jewelry designs. At one point I spent weeks searching for a portable anvil so that I could work with shaping wire into pendants and charms.[22]

After grad school, I continued on the jewelry making train and added in sewing, even though I hadn't touched a sewing school since my middle school Home Ec class. On a whim I decided I wanted to learn how to make art quilts and art dolls so that I could combine my sewing, embroidering, and jewelry making skills. The stress of a tenure track job was even more than the stress of grad school, hence the increased complexity of my creative endeavors. During this time I started making purses as well. At one point I even had an entire room dedicated to fabric, sewing supplies, and beads.[23] Around this time was when I decided that I wanted to bring my academic interests into my creative pursuits and decided to make a series of goddess quilts.[24] The goddesses were modeled after mid-century pin-up girls and surrounded by various symbols. For some of them, I embroidered their bodies to create a type of goddess pin-up patch

---

[21] As I've gotten older I have regularly created new creative challenges for myself, including the impulsive decision to participate in the 2022 Nanowrimo challenge out of which these meditations grew.

[22] I still have that anvil as a reminder of this moment in my creative life. Also, I love art supplies and tools and hate getting rid of them on the off chance I might need them again one day.

[23] Some would call this a studio, and in reality it was. However, in my fear of accepting the label of Creative or Artist, I simply called it my supply storage room.

[24] I now realize that this shift was my first movement toward a profession focused on creativity.

that was affixed to the art quilt. For others I hand painted fabric and then cut out body parts to assemble the goddess on the quilt. I was asked to hang the quilts in the café of the local Barnes and Noble as part of their featured artist series. Even though I didn't claim the title of Artist, I jumped at the chance to show off my work.

Fast forward to my whimsical desire to learn to paint during COVID lockdown. At the time the impetus for choosing this form of expression was because, "I'm not a painter but I've always wanted to paint." I said this all the time and truly believed it. I was far into my painting journey before I realized how much painting in various forms had snuck into my life over the years. However, I still didn't consider myself a Creative. In fact, when I would talk about my painting endeavors, I would proudly say to anyone who would listen, "I'm a professor. I love dabbling in these things, but I'm not a Creative." I still believed that artistic talent was a prized commodity meted out to only a select few, and I missed that line when the talents were being handed out. Even though I didn't know it at the time, the moment I opened the door to embracing my creativity is the moment I accepted the title of Creative and moving away from that of Professor.

Meditation 2
Find your Clicks

What are the things that you value or are important to you
but which you don't allow yourself to enjoy?

The first edition of *Ms. Magazine* had a fascinating article about the Click – that moment when something shifts in your perception, and you realize that you deserve more or can be more or experience some other type of personal empowerment.

My creative clicks started happening as soon as I allowed myself to dare think about centering creativity in my life. Since I loved creating and everything about it, why did I treat it as something that I didn't deserve? Why did I punish myself by always putting my creative time further and further into the future? I could respond with the easy answer and reference those childhood messages about work and what counts as work, and that was definitely part of the problem. The bigger problem, however, was me and how I valued, or didn't value me.

CLICK

For most of my life I believed I wasn't a Creative because I didn't have the credentials – either academic or talent. I'm not saying these are valid points or even that I still believe them, but they were part of the narrative I created to fool myself and continually devalue this aspect of my life. I am a first generation college student, and I like to joke that no one ever told me I could stop earning degrees, which is why I have so many. I began my educational career after a slight detour, meaning I started classes a semester later than my peers. As a girl who was a good student and who received good grades in math and science, I was strongly encouraged to pursue studies in Engineering. I was also good in writing and English but those were still considered traditional feminine pursuits and of lower value. I didn't know enough about myself at the time to push for studying what I wanted to do and happily went along with the suggestions of others and started Engineering classes.

The classes, especially my drafting class, were interesting at first. Additionally, I was forced[25] to spend hours in the artist supply section of the bookstore to purchase my necessary supplies.[26] I had never been in a classroom where the desks were drafting tables, which made coming to class feel like an exciting experience. An interesting side note is that at the time, the early 80s, you were still allowed to smoke in classrooms, so each drafting table came with an attached ashtray. Those easily accessible ashtrays meant that the classroom was usually filled with smoke and smelled exactly like how you would imagine decades of old cigarette smoke coupled with an overabundance of teenage boys would smell. After the first few weeks, I realized that maybe drafting wasn't as fun as I thought. Sure, I got to draw things and mess around with all my fun drafting tools, but figuring out how to calculate roof angles and draw lots of straight lines got boring rather quickly. The only real thing of substance I remember from those classes is that concrete is the substance you walk on, and cement is the binding agent. I still cringe whenever I hear someone talking about their cement sidewalk. In my head I scream, "No, just no." Instead of taking the time to figure out what I wanted to study, I dropped out for several years. Even though I loved learning and books and those drafting tools, I didn't value and/or trust myself enough to find out what I wanted to study.

---

[25] "Forced" here should be read as I willingly jumped in and happily spent my time dinking around.

[26] In an interesting bit of synchronicity I still have the t-square I purchased at that time and use it on a daily basis. As Kenneth Burke would say, I anticipated myself.

CLICK

After several arbitrary jobs and many nights of enjoying my early 20s[27] where I would stay out all night, come home for a quick shower, and show up fresh, if not still a bit drunk, for that day's job. I eventually returned to college, graduated, and started my professional life. However, that inability to value myself fully kept following me all the way through my life journey. I allowed my success to be defined by those external markers deemed relevant by society. I had letters, lots of letters, after my name. I had a professional career with a job secured by tenure. I owned a home and a car and an embarrassing number of shoes and purses. I wasn't rich but I had enough money for the occasional splurge. For all intents and purposes I had value. Don't get me wrong, those tangible and intangible things do have value, and I appreciate them and the privileges that come with them. However, somehow between those childhood moments of freely creating and becoming a successful adult, I had not only let myself be defined by my career, but I had also let my career control much of what I did. I did this even though I always felt lost and restless, wondering what else there might be.

CLICK

After my middle school art classes, I never stepped foot into an art class again. In eighth grade I was plucked from the masses of my classmates and fast tracked into college prep classes – the serious classes where you studied big theories and did "important things" without wasting time or energy on trivial things like painting and

---

[27] I am forever grateful that this period occurred before cell phones with their ability to document every stupid thing you do and say.

drawing.[28] In college, once I returned and got down to the business of earning a degree, I knew I wanted to go to grad school so I focused on taking classes that let me read good books and help me look like a well-rounded student prepared to continue their studies. I took the LSAT before the GRE and started getting recruited by law schools. After law school, I spent a few years practicing law and being on the partner track so I barely had time to eat, let alone create. I then entered my doctoral program where creating finally re-entered my life, but only as an outlet for stress.

An interesting aside here is that I still have yet to step foot into a formal art class. I've watched hundreds of YouTube videos and have taken a few online classes and certification trainings. Despite this over the years I have created untold number of items across a variety of media. You would think this fact alone would seem to qualify me at the very least as a Creative and arguably also as an Artist. However, in the narrative of creativity, these sorts of things are not the things that count – unless of course you are one of the lucky few who hit the creative lottery and are struck by the artistic lightning bolt of recognition and acceptance.[29]

CLICK

"Creative pursuits are only of value when they have a commercial pay off" -- I didn't realize how much I believed this until the click moment where I decided to toy with the thought of allowing more creativity into my life. Part of the commercialization of creativity rests in the myth of scarcity that surrounds it. According to this myth, only a few individuals in any life time are graced with the creative gene and allowed to advance to being "true" artists. Everyone else is just a dabbler or their bastard cousin, the artisan.

---

[28] To be perfectly clear, I don't believe this rhetoric. In fact I actively disavow these messages and am merely repeating them here for narrative purposes.
[29] I'm talking about you Kandinsky.

True art is a thing of torture for which you must starve and work hard and toil for years, or even a lifetime, before advancing to the next level. Think about how much awe and mesmerization we relegate to the story of Van Gogh's ear – he was so committed to his art that he tortured himself. Of course, this is all bullshit -- complete and utter bullshit, but bullshit that runs very deep. Van Gogh suffered from a number of mental disorders as well as struggling with substance abuse, which likely contributed to his self-mutilation.

CLICK

For me, all of these click realizations were especially interesting because I had always said that there are thousands of actors and singers who have amazing talent but simply aren't in the right place at the right time to advance to the next level. This doesn't mean they are any less talented than those whose names are well-known. It simply means they hadn't won the right lottery yet. However, I never applied that same mindset to my own creative pursuits – that damn lack of self-valuing again.

I want to be all sappy here and say that when the clicks started happening, I heard music playing and angels singing and the clouds parting to allow sun to shine down on me. Maybe that feeling was just the result of being cooped up in lockdown, but also, it kinda did feel like that. It felt like I was getting access to some secret knowledge. The golden ticket to a golden lifestyle. It was lockdown so I comforted myself by reminding myself that no one needed to know if suddenly I shifted my primary focus from the business of my work to the pleasure of my creativity, my art. I finally let myself use the "a" word about what I was doing. I was creating art. I was an Artist. An unexpected but glorious bonus of thesee click moments was that embracing my inner artist and letting her out demanded new art supplies. I told myself I would only find a small acrylic set and a few canvases, and I really believed it. Then I remembered my fondness for wandering the aisles of Dick Blick. While I couldn't venture into the physical store yet, the online store provided an equally satisfying wandering experience. On a whim I signed up for a Buddha painting class and deepened my foray into painting. I also begin adding at least three creative tasks to my daily task list, because even though my clicks had happened, the full realization and acceptance and embodying of the click would take some time yet.

Meditation 3
Painting Buddha

What fears or other things are holding you back from
pursuing those things that feed your soul?

As cliché as it may sound, the first time I painted Buddha was a transformative experience. I found myself, perhaps for the first time ever, embracing creativity and losing myself to its transformative lull.

Even though I'm not Buddhist, I first became interested in the study of Buddhism after taking a Religions of the East course in college – college the second time around when I took classes that allowed me to read good books. Raised in an evangelical Christian based church that focused heavily on the God of Job and religious beliefs of retribution, I wandered away from the church and organized religion in my teens, even though I continued to believe in the existence of a god and the necessity of doing good. Buddhism, with its acknowledgement of the sufferings of the world and its emphasis on mindful approaches to existence, made sense to me. I let my gut lead me to read works by the Dalai Lama, Thich Nhat Hanh, Pema Chödrön, and whoever else crossed my path. I also started a small collection of Buddha figurines, so painting the Buddha didn't seem like an odd step in my journey of discovering how to embrace my compassion and creativity.

During the lag time between ordering my art supplies and receiving them, I spent my days researching and reading about painting processes. When I reflect on this time, it's interesting because I was already following my artist's intuition. I don't remember ever affirmatively saying this out loud, but I knew that I didn't want to get wrapped up in learning "proper" painting techniques and processes. Over the years I had heard so many stories of people losing their creativity during the process of earning their Master of Fine Arts degree that I must have internalized the message to avoid these things. Instead, I found myself gravitating toward various forms of intuitive painting where the emphasis is on the process, not the final product. In hindsight, this makes sense. In my teaching practice, I spend significant amounts of time helping students reflect on their own processes in order to better understand who they are how and what they are learning. For assignments, I always emphasize that content is more important than form and spend countless numbers of hours mentoring students that it's ok to not have a specific format to fill while also encouraging them to embrace the opportunity to be creative.[30]

There are many different approaches to and understandings of intuitive painting. Even though I didn't have a conscious definition of it in those early Buddha days, my intuition, once again, had me covered. For me, intuitive painting is the process of allowing the canvas to reveal itself to you, letting it tell you what it wants to be. The process of getting there, the building up of layers is not just a practice in painting, but a meditative practice through which you come to know more about yourself. The canvas serves as a metaphor for your life. Its physical presence and your interaction with it is an embodiment in self-care and compassion. As you work around the canvas your eyes move left to right and up down; your hand dances around the surface leaving trails of paint everywhere it touches; without conscious effort you find yourself not worrying about the stress of life or work or even the painting. You are in the moment. Intuitive painting, especially in the early phases of a painting, provides a space where you can return to the play of childhood and

---

[30] Yes, I fully grasp the irony of me not doing what I was encouraging them to do.

not worry about outcomes or any of the other things that plague our adult lives.

I started my Buddha painting journey filled with excitement, and if I'm being honest, some trepidation. I still wasn't claiming the Artist title and was only dancing around the thought of claiming the title of Creative. Painting Buddha also meant painting a face, which at the time seemed impossible. However, in the spirit of living into my new embracing of allowing myself time for creative pursuits and being compassionate with myself, I took a deep breath and ripped open the plastic wrapping on the canvas.[31] I didn't realize at the time that according to the mythology of painting practices, I should have been frightened of or intimidated by the white expanse of the blank canvas. To me, the blank canvas represents the possibilities and promises of hope and aspirations.

In my flurry of art supply shopping I had ordered a wooden box set of supplies with a lid that could double as an easel. I set it up on a mid-century typewriter table, laid out my paints and took another deep breath. Lots and lots of deep breathing moments happened in those early painting days. I didn't realize it in the moment, but I was already approaching my painting time as an act of meditation. Eventually I would create a ritual that intentionally opens a meditative space for creativity as part of my painting practice, but more on that later.

I chose a purple oil pastel stick and wrote: peace, love, and happiness to begin the process and affirmatively interrupt the white expanse of canvas. I added a couple spirals and hearts for extra flourish. I didn't appreciate it at the time, but I now realize that even in that early learning phase, I was already finding my own flourishes and twists

---

[31] I still love the experience of removing the plastic from a new canvas. The sound and sensations feel like a rush of dopamine.

to add to my paintings.[32] The next step was adding blocks of color around the canvas to begin building up layers. I squirted seven or eight different color options on my palette, grabbed a brush, and started painting squares of color all around. Engaging in this process of simply placing random colors in random places was the first time I experienced entering that meditative state that intuitive painting can generate. By the time I was done with that first session I was surprised to learn that I had spent over an hour at the canvas. I remember marveling at how light and stress free I felt for the first time in ages. I texted a few friends about the experience and joked that I might have a new painting obsession.[33] I think I was worried they would discourage me or ask how I could find time to paint with all the work I had to do or any of those other self-imposed criticisms we subject ourselves to. To my surprise every single friend expressed joy and happiness for me. In those early days of embracing my creativity, telling someone this secret felt like a tremendous risk.

The remainder of my Buddha painting practice wasn't always smooth. Even though I fully believed in the premise of process over product, I still had that niggling little working class voice/critic telling me I had to make something good, whatever that means. I spent hours upon hours worrying about the facial features and how to get them to look "right." I struggled with how much paint I was "supposed" to use. I now realize that I was putting too much paint on my brush at one time, resulting in thick layers that not only took too long to dry but ended up looking rather flat. I watched the video about how to paint the nose at least 20 times. I read though other students' comments trying to find clues but I never did. Despite this, I somehow figured it out. I say somehow, but that downplays my

---

[32] Spirals and hearts can now be found in all of the under layers of my paintings and also appear in many of the final versions as well.
[33] It was a joke but also a glimpse of my future as my house currently has painting supplies in nearly every room.

contributions. I put a lot of work into the process and learned along the way that I could and should trust myself more.

In the process of adding final touches to Buddha, I decided to add in some washes of color by dipping my brush in paint then in water so the paint was very thin and would literally wash over the design. At one point, I decided to deepen the shadow under Buddha's right eye and ran a line of blue wash over the area. I then jumped to the top of Buddha's head and added in some more blue wash. I think I got interrupted or something and stepped away from the canvas for what turned out to be a couple hours. When I returned, I realized that in laying the wash under the eye, I must have pushed too hard on the brush, and the paint dripped down. My reaction upon initially seeing this was an oh, crap, what have I done moment. I then realized the drips looked like tears, which was fitting. I also realized that in addition to leaving all of my inner critic fears and concerns on the canvas, I had also left all of my pandemic fears and anger on the canvas.

Because I used so much paint on the brush, many of those early layers are completely buried in my final Buddha who I have affectionately and aptly named Pandemic Buddha. In my current paintings, I love letting those early layers show through and will often leave sections of the canvas deliberately untouched so those layers are fully visible. For Pandemic Buddha, I kind of like that those layers are buried. I know they are there. I think of them now, as a reminder of the fears and concerns I brought to that early canvas and that were left on it. Those fears and concerns, even though they were annoying at times and kept me locked into my box of comfort, served me well. They helped me succeed and in their own way they protected me. However, in their comfort, they also constrained me. Leaving them on the canvas and hanging that canvas on the wall – Pandemic Buddha is looking at me from across the room as I write this – was my first step in practicing self-compassion on the canvas.

When I look at the canvas now, I can enjoy the final Buddha, but I also am reminded of how far I have come.

Since finishing that Buddha I have lost count of how many more Buddhas I have painted. I have branched out into other subjects as well, including a series of goddesses on 36" x 40" canvases. Intuitive painting has become a necessary part of my life. More than a hobby, more than a meditation practice, it is the force that feeds my soul.

Meditation 4
Inner Dialogue

What are the things that tend to provoke your inner
critic and send you into a spiral of self-criticism?

The shift in perspective that happens when you allow yourself to embrace creativity and make it at least make as important as work is tremendous.[34] When you achieve this perspective, you can silence your inner critic or at least shift the dialogue to something more positive.

When I first shifted my perspective closer to embracing my creativity, I found myself feeling giddy. Each time I picked up my paintbrush I giggled. After a writing jag where I didn't worry about if what I was writing sounded academic enough, I felt lighter than air. It was as if I had unlocked some secret reservoir of joy.

I began the process of making this shift by adding creative tasks to my daily To-Do lists. I found that shifting how I framed creative moments helped me shift my perspective. By thinking of creative moments as tasks and not just hobbies, I found it easier to make time for them throughout the day instead of leaving them for after my "work." Even though equating creative pursuits with tasks may seem like a step backward, I believe it was a pivotal part of the larger shift I needed to allow myself time to create.[35] I divided my time between getting the business of "work" done and taking breaks to create. I wish I had a magic wand and could make this type of

---

[34] Every day I move closer to saying it is more important than work.
[35] I've since moved past needing to equate moments to create as tasks.

approach to everyone's workday the norm. I truly believe that allowing time for creativity ends up creating more time in the day. It seems counterintuitive, but allowing your mind to rest and flow however it wants opens up mental space for other things.[36]

This is not to say that moving toward embracing my creativity and accepting the title of being a Creative was all roses and puppy dogs and unicorns and rainbows – although wouldn't that world be a fun world to create in? Every time I approached a canvas or piece of watercolor paper or whatever substrate I was working on in the moment I felt nervous. I'm not sure how to fully describe it, but it was a mix of fear and uncertainty coupled with a heavy dose of imposter syndrome. To help move me past these frozen moments, I called on my knowledge of meditation and closed my eyes to take a few deep breaths. Even though the fear often lingered, my Irish stubbornness usually was able to overcome it enough for me to start creating.

Today I continue to embody this practice as it helps to center me in the moment and serves as a tangible break from the busyness of work. The ritual of pausing before painting allows me to shift more fully into creative mode. At times I'll light a candle or incense. Sometimes I will chant or read a poem out loud. I do whatever I am called to do in the moment as a way of reminding myself that what I am doing is an act of meditation, a practice in self-care, a moment of self-compassion, and not merely another task to be rushed through and completed. There are still those moments when I get caught up in worrying about the final outcome of a painting, but I try not to let them take control of the situation. When I feel these worries creeping in, I try to live into the moment and ask myself what are you really worried about here? This approach also means

---

[36] There is a growing body of research on this phenomenon. One of my favorite books on the subject is "The Awakened Brain" by Lisa Miller, Ph.D, Random House, 2021.

that at any given moment I have several paintings in progress lying around the studio, and if I'm being honest, around the house. I currently have four canvases lying against various walls in my living rooms waiting for their final touches, not to mention the many more that have taken up residence in the studio. I like to think of these canvases as friends that are staying for an extended period of time until they figure out their next posting in life.

As a child I was a precocious redhead with freckles, an insatiable curiosity about the world and how things worked, and probably a bit too much book knowledge for my own good. While I had friends, I was also too much for most kids, and probably most adults as well. I ended up spending a lot of time alone, and now realize that I was a loner before loners were necessarily a thing. I was constantly hopping on my bike to go explore. Thankfully I grew up before the era of helicopter and snow plow parents, meaning I would often have long stretches of time when I was left on my own. I lived in a city so there was always a park that needed to be explored or an abandoned building that might yield some sort of glorious find. I also lived close to the railroad tracks in a city that served as a major switching hub for cross-country trains.[37] I loved going to the tracks and walking up and down them looking for interesting rocks and other detritus. As an adult I reflect back on these times and wonder why no one ever stopped me. Some days I would be joined by friends, but we were mostly left to our own devices. In fact, the only time I ever remember being kicked off of a property was the time my friend Jimmy and I wandered into a grove of trees that were begging to be climbed. They were on the grounds of a company that packaged herbs and spices and must have been part of the crops they grew. We were simply yelled at and told to get moving without

---

[37] Interesting side note: my grandfather was a train engineer who worked himself up to the top spot before retiring. He would often take me to visit the trains and let me "drive" one and of course blow its horn. He was also a living example of Irish stubbornness in action.

anything else happening to us or anyone asking why we were out riding our bikes without any adults.[38]

Throughout these episodes, my inner dialogue, like most inner dialogues, provided a way for me to make sense of the world around me and help me figure out my place in it. As a child this inner dialogue was mostly consumed with commenting on all of the cool things I encountered during the day. On those many, many days when my precociousness overcame me and I was grounded yet again, my inner dialogue would run through the lists of things that were wrong with the world and the ways that I would make them better when I was an adult. I wish I could say that my inner dialogues continued in that way, but like all children I was growing and maturing. Like many girls, part of that maturation process involved becoming increasingly aware of the myriad messages surrounding me and that dictated how I should look and act as a girl on her way to becoming a woman. Just like those spoken and unspoken messages about the norms of working-class life, the spoken and unspoken messages about the norms of femininity run deep and hold a lot of power.

The first time I remember being conscious of the power of these norms was at a sleepover. Three of us were playing Twister, and my way of playing was to try to adopt the craziest twists and turns I could. I was naively enjoying myself with some semblance of a pretzel pose when the other two made that horrible noise that's a blend of a cluck and a tsk. Jenny, who would later become my mean girl nemesis, said, "Terri, what the hell are you doing? You look like a drunk crab who is about to fall over." I started to laugh and then looked over at Jenny and whoever else was playing. They were both bending over with their feet on two different colors and their hands

---

[38] Although I did end up getting grounded after this episode. One of my grandpa's neighbors worked at the company. She recognized my red hair and reported me to him.

in front of them. They looked like they were getting ready to tie their shoes, definitely not like a drunken crab. Jenny's verbal shaming of me was just loud enough that everyone else at the party heard and on cue laughed. Thus was born, Peggy, my inner critic.

Peggy has stayed with me all these years and can be quite the little nagging annoyance at times.[39] In times when I am overly stressed or feeling especially vulnerable, Peggy likes to sidle up and whisper horrible things to remind me of my lesser than status. I know that ultimately Peggy as my inner critic is a form of self-protection. If I monitor myself, see myself through the eyes of all the Jennys in the world, then I can either correct myself before they do or prepare myself for the inevitable backlash I will face. I understand this. I teach and talk about this stuff all the time. A significant portion of my academic career has been dedicated to theorizing the underlying sources of such behavior, identifying the ways it plays out in our daily lives, and naming it as a way to help others move beyond it. Of course, just because I understand and can explain it doesn't mean that I don't still fall prey to it.

Not surprisingly when I shifted my perspective to embracing creativity and let myself start painting, a whole new field of criticism opened up for Peggy. All the time I spent struggling with Buddha's face was a byproduct of Peggy's work. If we believe the scarcity myth that there is only so much creativity in the world and that only a lucky few are allowed to be creative, then we must of course struggle when we create. Working alongside this myth is the commodification of creativity or the task mindset which mandates that you must always be creating some tangible thing. The end product is the important thing, not the process. These messages, like

---

[39] While some people would call her a bitch, I don't because I firmly believe that the word bitch is the key title holder in the rhetoric of shaming words tossed at women. As such, I openly embrace my own bitchiness and encourage other women to do so as well.

the others I've discussed, surround us and run deep. Even if we don't realize it, we've all internalized them. I am confident that part of my resistance, hesitancy, failure, to embrace my creativity for so long was connected to my internalization of these messages. I was acting on the fear that unless I produced something glorious I was a failure, and as a busy professional I don't have a lot of extra time so why waste time doing something that is a failure. I don't believe these things, but at the same time I think I did for a very long time. I bought into the mindset that art was something that only a very few could do and that everything else was lesser than, craft or hobby but not art. Since I wasn't an artist, by definition I couldn't create art.

Without necessarily being conscious of it, I took comfort in this approach. By letting Peggy hold me back, I didn't have to worry about the Jennys of the world and their shaming words. I could live a wonderful life with my hobbies and crafts and be happy. Don't get me wrong, I was happy and a success and all those other things we put value in. However, I was also always searching for something else, a part of me that was missing. The thing that I didn't even know I could do or that I must do, and the thing that I now can't imagine not doing – painting, throwing paint on canvases and letting what will be, be.

Meditation 5
Fear and Resistance and Self-compassion

What are the things that scare you and hold you back
from achieving the success you deserve?

Fear and resistance and self-compassion. These are the things I think about a lot lately. Perhaps I've always thought about them but didn't realize that's what they were.

Diving into intuitive painting allowed, perhaps forced, me to identify and name the connections between fear and resistance. I specifically had to admit and name the myriad ways that fear creates resistance which can be crippling in its deleterious effects. I firmly believe that the primary, perhaps the only, way to break through this resistance is with intentional acts of self-compassion. When I say self-compassion in this way I think of it not as mere self-care, but instead as true love, concern, and empathy for you, including an acknowledgement of your particular underlying issues creating fear.

I often wonder if the human condition is defined in part by fear. What I mean by that is I wonder if fear is innate or is it learned? Even as I write that, I know that this binary is an oversimplification, at least in part. I think to understand the phenomenon better, we have to think about categories of fear. I'm sure that someone or many someones have devoted their lives to delineating out the various types of fears experienced by humans as well as the responses created to deal with them. For example, we know that the fight, flight, or freeze reaction to a fear inducing stimulus is a natural cognitive response designed to protect ourselves. Likewise we know that parents will take extraordinary action to save their children when they are confronted with danger. The psychology and physiology of these types of responses would fall into the innate type of fear and are fascinating in their own right. What I'm thinking about here, however, are those fears that we create. The ones that our inner critic loves to pester us about.

When does fear morph into resistance? I've spent a lot of my professional life thinking through the connections between power, discourse, and knowledge. I have been specifically interested in unraveling the social mandates that dictate how we are supposed to walk through our lives. I have also been interested in interrogating how we come to know what things are and aren't acceptable as well as how we communicate about them. To simplify it even more, how are behavioral mandates communicated to us and how do we take them up to communicate them to others and to ourselves? Much of my research has revolved around the social rules that mandate acceptable and unacceptable ways for women to behave in American society. For example, we are told that we can be empowered and lead the life we want to lead, yet if we are too empowered and dare to speak out against someone in power, we are often put into our place. A typical response to such a daring woman being called a bitch or for those who are afraid of "bad" words, a shrew.[40]

As a child of the 70s I remember being surrounded by second wave feminist messages that women could do whatever men did. When I think about this time I always think about the commercial for Enjoli cologne. The ad features one woman in three different roles – businesswoman, housewife, lover. She acts out each role while singing, "I can bring home the bacon. Fry it up in pan, And never let him forget he's a man because I'm a woman." My friends and I would chant this song while walking around the playground at

---

[40] When I say typical, I am not saying I agree with this response.

recess.[41] The ad itself has many problems, none the least of which is the fact that it glamorizes the 24/7 work lives of many women who are wives and mothers. However, the ad also seems to imply that bringing home the bacon is something desirable, so desirable that we should buy Enjoli perfume to make it happen. So why then would a woman living up to that ideal be considered a bitch?[42] And what does all of this have to do with fear and resistance and self-compassion?

I think the connection occurs when I reflect on the disconnect between the messages I heard about who I could be and the messages I received when I tried to be empowered. I like being challenged and have yet to meet a challenge I'm not willing to take up. My love of reading coupled with my active inner life means that as a child, and even to some extent still today, I was always thinking about other things I could do and be. I wanted to be a teacher, a writer, an artist, a businesswoman (but not the Enjoli kind), and many other things I've forgotten over the years. To make my writing dreams happen I started sending off poetry to "Teen" and "Seventeen" magazines. Sometime during middle school my friends and I began to read these magazines religiously every month, and I became convinced that having a poem published in one of them would be the start of my glorious writing career. Through many moves I've lost the journals that housed my teenage attempts at poetry.[43] However, for some reason I still have some of those early form letter rejections. The interesting thing is that having my poetry rejected, even by form letter, didn't generate a fear of trying again. In fact, these rejections motivated me to try harder. I viewed the rejections as merely one more step in the process.

---

[41] I cringe now when I think back to the overt sexual imagery of the song and wonder at the adults who simply smiled at us as we sang away.
[42] This is a rhetorical question, but I also kinda want an answer.
[43] This is probably a good thing as I'm sure Peggy would have volumes of things to say about my precociously loquacious teenage self.

Somewhere along the journey I abandoned my quest to be published in "Teen" or "Seventeen" and picked up the fear commonly associated with rejections -- the fear of being thought lesser than, not worthy, silly, etc. It wasn't necessarily a conscious moment of feeling fear, and I doubt that I ever even acknowledged it as such. Instead I developed a resistance to memorializing my thoughts in poetry or other "formal" writings. Even as I'm writing this, I can feel vestiges of that fear and hear Peggy's whispers, "don't use that word. You've already used it too many times"; "does any of this really matter. Who is going to want to read this"; "don't you have real work you should be focusing on"; "who are you to say these things and haven't they already been said by people better than you". Peggy can be mean at times. But Peggy, as an embodiment of my fear, is protecting me, the same way my resistance to writing protects me.[44] Even though I'm focused in this moment on writing, that same fear and resistance extends to all of my creativity. If I don't do it, then I'm safe and secure. I may be sad and not fully realizing my potential, but I'm safe.

To move beyond the safety of resistance requires not just a shift in perspective but perhaps more importantly, radical self-compassion. Earlier I distinguished self-compassion from self-care, even though practicing self-compassion is an act of caring for yourself. To me it feels like the concept of self-care has been watered down and reduced to spa days and mani/pedi dates and drinking fancy coffee or wine with your friends. It's more of a one off thing you to do to show you love yourself. It's a thing you can buy with its pink and gold and glitter packaging. It's a performance you put on to show how empowered you are.[45] Don't get me wrong, I love all the products associated with self-care ideals and will rarely turn down an offer to get coffee or wine with a friend. My frustration is with how

---

[44] A related kind of fear is why I stuck with my role as a professor so long. It was a safe option.

[45] Yes, I might have some feelings about the whole self-care industry.

the products are removed from any sort of reflection or deep thought. When I talk about self-compassion, I mean more than these acts of self-indulgence. Self-compassion is a way of being in the world where you embody empathy for yourself, accepting the total package of you without trying to push down the negative or bad things.

To practice self-compassion is a difficult task and one that takes ongoing practice and intentionality. It takes strength and patience and endurance. It's messy and often leads to thoughts and realizations that can make you feel yucky. To practice self-compassion requires honesty, complete and utter honesty. It demands that you acknowledge all of your feelings and thoughts, not just those that are happy and perky. I believe that sitting with those yucky feelings and thoughts are the most important part of self-compassion. By working through the things you don't want to think about, you uncover the things you've been hiding from yourself, the things you might not have even realized you knew or thought. All of this also means that practicing self-compassion is hard, really hard. Living with fear and resistance is much easier.[46] Even though you don't experience as much of life, you're safe and secure. And this is the primary reason why radical self-compassion is necessary. You have to keep pushing past the safety and security of the known because it's only then that you will find the glory of the unknown.

All of this is ultimately why that question about what my life would look like if I embraced creativity threw me for such a loop. I was forced out of my zone of safety and security and had to reconcile with my own reality. I had to admit that the time for change had come a long time ago, and it was well past time for me to accept that change. Even though I started the self-work class as a response to being in COVID lockdown, I think that even without lockdown this

---

[46] Trust me, I've been doing it for years.

moment of reckoning would have happened. It would have likely occurred in a different form or with a different prompt, but I believe embracing my inner Creative is something I had been moving toward for a long time.

The big thing that staying in my safety and security zones was hiding was that despite my professional and personal success, I was intensely sad and unhappy. In retrospect I am pretty confident I was struggling with a few years of clinical depression as well. It was easy to ignore all of this though, because I was able to display those tangible markers of success. Opening myself up to my creative side opened the proverbial can of worms – once the seal was opened it could never be put back together. Radical self-compassion, the thing I teach and preach whenever I can, required me to sit with these feelings in order to unpack them. Why was I sad? Why wasn't I satisfied? What did I want? How could I move past surviving and begin thriving? How was I going to make it happen? And even as I began asking these questions, I heard Peggy prompting me with other questions, "why does it matter"; "why are you complaining"; "others have it much worse than you"; and the killer question that almost stopped me from making the change, "you have a position that others would dream of and fight for, how can you give it up and what about all those people you will be disappointing?"[47]

---

[47] Peggy is intense. During my first round of edits, she creeped in many different times, trying to convince me to abandon this project.

Meditation 6
Perfect is Boring

What would your life look like if you allowed yourself
not to worry about perfection?

I have a shirt that says, "Perfect is boring." I don't remember how
or why I bought it, but it's become one of my favorites. The
message is an important one to consider.

While it often seems that perfection is an ideal goal, ultimately it is
an unnecessary and empty pursuit. Who gets to decide what is
perfect and why is it up to them? Life is messy. Maybe I'm biased
because my life has been a messy and complicated journey. Yet
whenever I reflect on that journey, the times that are now the most
memorable were the biggest messes in the moment. At the same
time, however, there is something intriguing about seeking
perfection. There must be since it often seems like so many people
have the achievement of some state of perfection as their goal.

I wonder if the pursuit of perfect is less about seeking perfection and
more about avoiding failure. Fear of failure can be debilitating. This
makes sense since as a society we valorize winners. We praise those
who are able to rise to the top and somehow come out victorious.[48]
Likewise, we scorn and pity those who are unable to rise to the
occasion and end up lost amongst the masses. Logically, this type of
system isn't sustainable – there can only be one winner in any
endeavor, meaning that the masses, the many, are losers. Are we

---

[48] This is why the rhetoric of the whole pull yourself up by the bootstraps myth
continues to hold so much power.

really to believe and accept that most people are losers and therefore by definition lesser than? I'm not willing to make that concession.

Equally important, though, is the question of what is failure? Similar to perfection, who gets to decide and why is up to them? Let me illustrate this with an example from a paper I was grading today. The class in question is one focusing on community organizing and networking. As an experiential learning class, the goal is to have students working with situations and individuals in a real-world simulation, not just the usual classroom setting of lectures followed by tests and assignments. My focus this year in the class is having them design an educational campaign about domestic and relationship violence followed by a supplies drive to support the YWCA. After the first few classes of set up and introduction, the schedule for the class is blank. Students must come together and organize themselves into a team. While I am a part of the classroom, I don't determine the day's agendas or needs. Instead I work with students as part of the team as they set goals and tasks to move closer to their goals. One of the most difficult lessons that students have to grapple with in the class is learning to trust themselves and set their own schedule. They have become so used to having classes with detailed plans spelled out in advance that they forget how to operate without a plan. They become convinced that as long as they plan everything out they will achieve perfection. When confronted with the task of making their own schedule, they become immobilized with fear.

I know that this type of class set up is scary for many students. I understand the fear that comes with not knowing exactly what you have to do to succeed, but that is where the situation gets interesting. In the modern educational system, success or perfection is tied to grades. The system is based on a consumer transaction model. While we say the product of this model is an education, the real product is the letter grade. The basic transaction is that you pay for an education, the teacher imparts their knowledge to you, you repeat the knowledge back to them, and then you receive a grade. We put a lot of value into these grades -- honor societies, scholarships, advanced placement credits. We honor the top grade earners by bestowing them with the labels of valedictorian and salutatorian. This value system starts in kindergarten, so as children mature, the system becomes second nature to them.[49] They are told how good they are when they bring home good grades. In effect, the grade then becomes a proxy for the self, with the value of the individual wrapped up in the value of the grade. Seeking these grades can become an obsession.[50] Students in college have been immersed in this system for much of their lives, so they know the ins and outs, the proverbial tricks of the trade. They know that if they follow all the rules, their success will be marked with the good letter grade they receive at the end of the semester. The closer they get to perfection, the higher the grade. However, is that good letter grade really the mark of educational success or perfection?

The interesting thing about the grade system is that the grade is completely removed from what it is supposed to stand for or represent. A letter grade is not indicative of what an individual has or hasn't learned. A letter grade simply marks an individual's ability to follow directions and complete assigned tasks. Learning occurs outside of these events and often doesn't fully happen until long after the class is over. For example, in my first English Composition class in college, I received a D on one of first papers. I loved writing and had never received any grade other than an A, so seeing a D was a complete shock and surprise. When I saw it I felt sad and mad simultaneously. At the end of class, I rushed to speak with the professor who gave me a detailed explanation for the grade – I had

---

[49] There's a whole rant waiting to burst out about how this model also creates compliant little worker drones.
[50] I speak from my own experience of feeling the need to collect As in order to feel complete.

misunderstood the assignment and while what I wrote was good it didn't meet the requirements. All I saw, however, was that glaring D and how that meant I wasn't a good student. Even though this event happened over 30 years ago, I still remember all the details of it even though I don't remember what I wrote about. I also remember the lesson I took from that experience. From then on, I always made sure to read the assignments and follow them.

Back to the paper I was grading, several students expressed a concern that their campaign would be a failure. Intrigued by their concerns and wanting to understand the depth of the problem I engaged the entire class in a discussion about what would constitute a failure. The concerns ranged from not being able to run a campaign in the time frame of the semester to not being able to reach enough people to not being able to change people's minds about domestic and relationship violence. We then talked about what a success would look like. I expected an equally vigorous conversation and instead was met with silence and looks of confusion. That's when I realized that the concern about failure was simply another debilitating fear, a fear grounded at least in part in not fully understanding the difference between failure and success. Their fear was at least in part a worry about not achieving perfection. What does success look like here? Is success defined by the creation and running of the campaign or by the process of working through trying to run a campaign? Is success limited to only one form? For me, this answer is much more difficult as I can see value in everything the class was doing. I honestly don't know that failure is even possible unless perhaps for someone who drops out of the class and never has the opportunity to grapple through the process.[51]

The real problem here, or at least a big part of it, is the equating of failure and success with something tangible, a product. In other

---

[51] Likewise, I don't know that perfection is even possible.

words, it's yet another byproduct of the consumerist mindset of the West. If we pay the right combination of money and work and sweat and whatever other tokens are demanded/required, we should be successful. I call bullshit. I also call bullshit on the whole concept of success and failure. I believe that we can take any situation that appears one way and twist it so that it appears the other way. With my students for example, let's say that they designed a campaign and got it up and running with posters and table tents and other sorts of materials flooding campus. According to their definition this would be a success. But what if no one bothers to look at the materials. Or, heaven forbid, what if another global pandemic happened causing the campus to shut down. We could then say that the campaign is a failure. Ultimately, the labels of failure and success are meaningless. They only have any value because we allow them to or think they have meaning. They exist because we let them exist.

All of this seems to be inherently connected to another aspect of fear. We fear not achieving perfection, so we don't take a chance. We never stop to think about what would happen if we succeed? That future possibility never seems to arise. For creativity, I see the fear of not achieving perfection in many ways -- the inability to start a project, the abandoning of a project midstream, the hours upon hours I spent trying to perfect the Buddha's face. It took me a long time to understand that the failure I so feared happening in my art was something I was creating and often something only I was seeing. Sometimes I will randomly post a picture of a work in progress on my social media. I'm always shocked at the things other see and the things I have failed to see in my work. Where I see a lack of perfection, others see art they want to own.

It seems that ultimately failure of perfection and success present another lesson in perspective – it all depends on how you look at it. I usually have at least one canvas in rotation that I consider a play canvas. Paint is expensive, and I hate to waste it. Often times, however, I will squeeze more paint onto my palette than I end up needing. Instead of trying to load it all onto the canvas in progress[52], I will use it on my play canvas. I consider these play canvases because they never start out with any intention other than to be a repository for extra paint. I approach these canvases in full intuitive mode following whatever thought first pops into my head. Sometimes it will be a word of inspiration. Sometimes I will paint hearts or spirals. Other times, I just paint circles. On days where I'm feeling especially feisty I will get my best Jackson Pollack on and fling paint at the canvas creating blobs and drips and splatters everywhere.[53] Inevitably there comes a point where I see the play canvas from a different perspective and realize I like what is happening on it. I see that the play has become the foundation for a Buddha or goddess or other subject. On the same wall as Pandemic Buddha is a Peace Buddha I painted. This Buddha's background began as one of these play canvases. In the final version it looks like Buddha is emerging from a graffitied wall. It looks intentional, even though it was not. The interesting question this prompts for me then is: is this painting a success or failure? It's on my wall so that would seem it is a success. However, it was intended to be a play canvas, which then lost its purpose or at least had its purpose redirected so isn't that failure? Does it really matter in the end?

Maybe this is why my Perfect is Boring shirt resonates with me so much. Perfection seems to be a form of success. Success, however, is also an end result. Once you reach it there is nothing else. Once you achieve perfection that's it. What else is left? Maybe the real success then comes in failing repeatedly so that you can keep striving to do more? And even then, who gets to decide and why?

---

[52] I learned my lesson after the days of painting Buddha with too much paint on my brush.
[53] This is also how more and more of my clothes end up with drops of paint on them in what seem the most random spots.

External vs. Internal Validation

Where and how do you seek validation?

For several years I have been interested in the phenomenon of personal validation, specifically why is the drive for external validation so strong in many people?

When I think of external validation I think of it as the need to have others affirm your existence, your value. Internal validation, by extension therefore, is affirming your own existence and value. What I find especially fascinating is how often external validation is valued more than internal.

The first time I reflected on this phenomenon was early in my teaching career during a commencement ceremony. On this campus, faculty sat in the first rows of the audience facing the stage, meaning we had a good view of the proceedings. We were organized by rank and years of service, and since I was a newer professor I was toward the back of the faculty rows. The speaker at the time was a governor, I can't remember if he was the sitting governor or a former one. I don't remember all of his speech, or any of the other speeches either.[54] The one thing I do remember, however, was the way he framed the importance of internal validation over external. He pointed out that if we place our emphasis on the values that others put us on, take their assessments of us over our own, we have to do this for both the positive and the negative. If my need to feel good about myself is dependent upon someone else telling me I'm good,

---

[54] Does anyone ever remember commencement speeches?

then when another someone else tells me I'm bad I have to give that the same weight as the good. This seems like such a simple premise, but of course sometimes the greatest insights are those that seem simple or basic.

Despite the simplicity of this premise; however, I often wonder why the thoughts of others weigh so heavily on us.[55] I don't know that I have the answer, or even if there is an answer. What I've been reflecting on, though are possible answers. The most obvious reason we seek external validation is likely connected to our desire to be liked by others. As humans we are communal by nature. Part of being in a community is being active in it by interacting with the others surrounding you, and part of interacting with others means liking some folks and not liking others. We first learn this lesson as children when we start making friends. We choose to be friends with those we like and avoid those we don't like. As we mature, our friend groups change as we become more selective in who we bring into our lives. We form friend communities around shared interests – cheerleading, theatre, sports teams, etc. However, anyone who has survived middle and high school also knows that groups are formed around social hierarchies – cool kids, rich kids, smart kids, goth kids, etc. Sometimes there is overlap between the groups, but as with most social hierarchies there are no formal rules. What is cool one week may be terribly passé the next. Wanting to be part of a desired group is a form of seeking external validation. We believe that by being in the desired group we become desired, and the status of this desirability is maintained by excluding those who are less desirable.[56]

As we continue to mature, we outgrow these school age cliques; however, we don't outgrow the desire to be part of a community. We also, often, don't outgrow the need for external validation. In

---

[55] I still fall prey to these kinds of worries, sometimes on a daily basis.
[56] We see these concepts repeated and reinforced to us throughout media and social media all the time.

fact, I would argue that as we move toward adulthood the need for external validation rises. By adulthood I mean not just chronological age but also the time of making your own life -- one that isn't defined by your parents and teachers. I think of this time as setting up your first home space, entering the work force[57], being responsible for yourself. These moments happen in phases, and you may not even realize they are happening until you are forced to in some manner. For me, the moment of realizing I had reached adulthood happened the first time I had a stomach bug in my apartment. I shared this apartment with a roommate, who had gone to work while I stayed home trying to manage my roiling stomach. During one especially intense wave of nausea, I knew that I needed to vomit and that it would happen soon. I gathered the energy to pull myself off the couch and started shuffling to the bathroom. I only made it a few steps before the vomiting erupted. I rushed the rest of the way to the bathroom, leaving a trail of vomit in my wake. When my stomach was emptied of everything, I cleaned up my face, brushed my teeth, and started to head back to the couch. Then I saw the vomit trail. I realized that no matter how nauseated I still felt, that was my mess, and I needed to clean it up.

One of the aspects of this phase in life is that you don't have a built in friend set. As a child you move from one cohort to another, all of which provide easy access to possible friends. Before you start school you have the kids in the neighborhood who you merely have to go outside to find. In grade school you have the kids in your class who sit by you and who you see daily who can be your friends. Many of these friends will follow you to middle and high school where you will also meet new possible friends. In college you will take classes and participate in clubs and organizations with people who become your friends based on your similar interests. The defining characteristic in all of these situations is you are surrounded by other

---

[57] Or for those who really love education, entering graduate school

people at the same phase in their lives as you and who are experiencing similar things as you at the same time. You have a veritable smorgasbord of people from which to choose your friends.

As an adult these pre-fab cohorts of possible friends don't automatically happen. Making friends becomes a tangible thing you have to make happen. Even if you are in a workplace where you are hired as part of a cohort of similar others, you are surrounded by myriad other people in different phases of their professional life and of different generations. In addition, you will confront people who like to keep their personal and professional lives separate. Making friends, therefore, can seem like a job in itself. When I first moved to South Bend, I was only planning on staying for a year since my position was a one year visiting professor gig. There were two other visiting professors in my building, so we became fast friends for the year. When I was offered and accepted a tenure track position, they had moved on, and I found myself feeling lost.[58] In moments like this, the need to feel propped up by random others, external validation, worms its way to the top as we want to be liked and feel like we belong.

The situation becomes even more complicated when we add in the prospect of living into our creativity. No matter how much I write or paint or otherwise delve into creative pursuits, there is a always a small part of me that worries about if what I am creating is good, even though I couldn't define good if I was forced to do so. Good is subjective, and what one counts as good for another will count as bad for another. I know this and preach it all the time. For example, I love abstract art even though I know that for many people abstract art looks like nothing more than globs of paint haphazardly thrown on a canvas. I can't force them to see what I do when I look at a

---

[58] I am happy to report that in the ensuing years I have made many wonderful friends here.

piece of abstract art. Why then, with my own creative pursuits, would I worry about if others think my work is good?

What I find interesting about the need and desire for external validation is why should we believe what someone else thinks about us over what we think about ourselves? Does some random stranger or even a close friend or family member know us better than we know ourselves? Why do we think that someone who isn't intimately aware of our needs, desires, and goals is better situated to determine if we are meeting them? How is someone who doesn't live in our body and walk through our daily lives able to fully evaluate if we are succeeding? And why would we care what they think? I ask these questions even as I struggle to find my own answers.

The person we need to look in the eye in the mirror every morning and every night is ourselves. Our validation should be the only one that matters. If I think I am doing something right, even if it doesn't make sense to anyone else, does that matter? Intellectually, I know this is the case but there is still that part of me that continues to question. When I first started reflecting on the concept of validation, I found myself asking a series of questions. I'm still seeking the answers, and maybe there are no answers. These are the questions I continue to ponder as I move closer to fully embracing my creativity and myself. What does it take to raise the value of internal validation to that of external? Or, to be even more daring, to completely replace external validation with internal? What would your life look like if you put as much time into pleasing yourself and meeting your own standards as you do into those of others? How would your life change if you didn't have to worry every day about what others think? What could you accomplish if you took all that energy and redirected it toward things that are important to you? What could you create? Who could you be?

Meditation 8
Persistence

In what areas of your life do you need to be more persistent?

Some days, I don't feel like creating in any format. Some days, like today, it's because I've already had a long day and am exhausted. Other days, though, there's a certain hesitation that keeps me from the page or the canvas.

I love creating and know that I feel more like myself when I carve out space for creative play. It's frustrating, therefore, when I don't feel like creating. I'm not really sure what the underlying cause of this feeling is, and perhaps there are multiple reasons. However, the last time this happened I sat with the discomfort of the feeling and tried to get to the bottom of it. I asked myself, what is really happening here? You love to paint and have some amazing works in progress in addition to having a plethora of blank canvases and papers you could use to start a new project. [59] The first response that flew to my mind was, "I'm just not feeling it. I don't know where to begin." As I sat a little longer, doubts and negative thoughts began flooding in. "The face on that goddess looks off, and I don't know how to fix it." "The colors on that abstract look off, and I don't know what to do to change it." "Watercolors are too messy, and I don't feel like setting up a new spot to play with them." "This essay is going in a weird direction from where I intended, and I don't know how to get it back on track." Each time I sit with this discomfort, the specific responses vary depending on the specific project or

---

[59] I literally asked the question out loud. Somehow it takes on more gravitas that way and requires a serious answer.

projects I'm working on at that moment, but the basic nature of them follow these same patterns. I'm at a middle or awkward spot in the creative journey and convince myself I'm stuck there.

I find thoughts like these interesting because I really do love creating. With painting, for example, even when it's a mess, I find myself getting lost in the meditative nature of the process. Attending to the moment, whether it is picking the colors I'm going to use and getting them onto my palette or working around the canvas creating marks and texture or even the simple act of rinsing the brush in water to remove any lingering paint pigment are all simple acts of mindfulness. When I can work myself past my resistance and show up at the canvas, each step of the process takes me further away from the stress of daily life and deeper into a meditative state. It is as if I become one with the canvas and can hear it telling me what it wants to be. When I am in this flow state, I intuitively respond to cues given by the canvas. I often find myself moving toward placing the brush on a section of the canvas and feel it being rejected or repelled. It's almost magical how it feels like a type of invisible barrier has appeared over this section of the canvas, protecting it from this particular brush stroke. The first few times this happened I was confused as to what was happening. As I became more comfortable with intuitive painting and with trusting my flow state, I began to realize how this was an embodiment or enactment of my connection to the process. I am always surprised when these moments happen. Surprised at both where the painting takes me in its development and surprised at the way the process makes me feel.

With writing, the intuitive flow appears differently. Writing flow happens when I allow myself to simply pour out whatever words or thoughts jump to mind without worrying about clarity or even if the thoughts make sense. This flow most easily occurs when I return to my old school approach and write with a pen on paper. My longtime favorite choice is yellow legal pads and black gel ink pens.[60] The process of putting words onto paper adds a physical element to the mental process of creating. A blank sheet of paper becomes covered with the squiggles and lines representing words. The scratching and scraping sound of the pen inscribing onto the paper becomes the white noise background soundtrack of the process. Without the prompts of a computer alerting me every time I spell a word wrong or make a grammar mistake, the temptation to edit while writing disappears. Even if I do decide I don't like something I have written, a simple line crossing it out eliminates it without deleting it, which is important because often those first thoughts that are too quickly eliminated end up being the best thoughts. The process of getting into writing flow differs from that of painting flow, but the end result of feeling as if I am coming out of a long meditative state is the same. It seems, therefore, that entering into this flow state would be something I would eagerly want to make happen.

When I reflect more deeply on my resistance to creating, I can see that the true issue is not the act of creating itself. The crux of the matter can be found by looking at those first responses that flew to my mind when I allowed myself to sit with this discomfort. Each response is a criticism of some aspect of the painting or writing, which in itself isn't a bad thing. An important part of the design process is being able to critically evaluate all of the components of the composition – whether that composition is created with paints or with words. The key aspect of my responses, however, rests in the second part of the statement, the section following the "and." The words may vary, but they all represent a form of self-doubt, a feeling of incompetency often accompanied with a sense of helplessness. Over the years I've written thousands of words in completed essays and articles. Many of these have been published and read by others.

---

[60] There's something comforting about the juxtaposition of dark ink on cheery yellow paper.

In the short time I've been actively painting, I've created hundreds of paintings of all sizes. I've had works commissioned and have sold some of the paintings that were simply canvases where I played around with paint. Clearly I have the technical skill and know how to fix an abstract whose colors are off or an essay which has moved in a new direction. While these "issues" may be the stated problem, they are actually like scapegoat problems, things I can hide behind to avoid looking deeper.

If I'm being honest with myself, the real problem is fear with a side of imposter syndrome. Still active deep down inside me is that little working-class girl who learned that getting a job and succeeding were the most important things to accomplish in life. There's that part of me that denied the need for creativity and only allowed it out after all the work had been done. There's the academic me who is aware that while I have a lot of credentials and lots of letters after my name, I don't have the "right" credentials for this type of work.[61] There's Peggy with her protective voice that comes out in the form of criticism. And if I'm being really honest, there's that part of me that fears failure, even as I don't know what failure would look like in terms of my own creativity. All of these fears are self-created. There's no one standing over me telling me that I cannot paint because I don't have the correct formal training. There's no one looking through the work I've completed, or not completed for the day, and determining if I've done enough to have earned a moment of creativity. The reality is that I could write and paint every single day for the rest of my life, and there is nothing forcing me to share those creations with anyone else, so how could they ever be deemed to be failures? Intellectually, I know all of these things. I say similar things to my students and coaching clients. Yet for some reason, I still have

---

[61] I could write a book about the myriad insidious ways the academy drives creativity out of you.

a hard time believing them. In other words, I have a hard time believing in myself.

Ultimately, the heart of the problem is that I don't have faith in myself. Even though I say the right platitudes and assure myself that, "Yes, I can do this," I don't believe it. I've put up a defensive block against myself. This is kind of messed up even as it's not surprising. Like everyone else, I am surrounded by all those messages dictating who and how I should be. I've spent a lifetime learning how to operate amongst these demands and have created ways to handle them. I have my good friend Peggy to help me protect myself from the damaging effects of these messages, even when I'm the messenger. Even though the feeling of achieving the flow state is so luxurious and calming, the defensive blocks pop up. Unlearning these ways of being and replacing them with different and better ones is a long process. It may be a process I never master and keep working on for the rest of my life. Maybe that's the main lesson I'm supposed to take away from all of this. It's not about mastering it but about figuring out how to live with it.

The interesting thing is that if I can find a tiny bit of strength to push past the resistance and move my ass to the canvas or the page, I inevitably find out I can do the things I said I couldn't a few minutes ago. I find that even though I was convinced that my flow state was an elusive illusion for the day, it found its way to me. The perfect example of this are these very words I'm writing now. I delayed tackling this today because I had a busy day in school and had to be in court. I was mentally and physically drained and probably feeling a little sorry for myself. The couch was calling me for a nap, and I was not feeling creative at all. I wanted to take a nap and turn on some mindless television show. Being the smart ass that I am I told myself, "Fine, I'll do the damn writing but I'm going to write about what a shit mood I'm in." And being the petulant child I can still sometimes be, I also said, "It's going to be super short and super crappy and then I'm going to drink wine." Now, here I am, and I even learned a little something along the way.

Meditation 9
Quitters Never Win?

When should you continue to persevere on a project and
when should you admit it's time to quit?

Quitters never win, and winners never quit." I hate this saying. I know it's supposed to be motivational and inspirational and all, but it's one of those things that make me cringe whenever I hear or read it.

I don't know the genesis of the saying and don't want to waste time researching it when there are so many other things calling on my time.[62] However, to me the saying first came onto my radar during the rise of the Yuppies and their no holds, make all the money era.[63] The whole focus of this ethos is that you can succeed if you want to and if you work hard enough. Implicit in this is that you must not quit, for quitting is not the way of winning. Even though I never consciously made the connection before, I'm pretty sure this concept was one of the things feeding into my resistance to quit being a professor. Somewhere deep down, I think I believed, or at least wanted to believe, that the trappings of my professional success were enough since they made me look like a winner.

The quitters never win mindset also reminds me of the pull yourself up by the bootstraps ethos of the American Dream, which is really

---

[62] One of the downsides of my quest to be a Renaissance man is that there's always some new subject or skill to master.

[63] At the height of this era I tended bar in a full on Yuppie place. It pretended to be a dive bar while it sold over priced mixed drinks and martinis. Centered behind the bar was a poster declaring: "He who has the most toys wins."

the American Myth. The American Dream approach sounds good on the surface, but when you start to think more deeply about it, it quickly falls apart. It misses the fact that not everyone begins from the same point or with the same access to resources. It misses all of the social and cultural and political factors that operate to keep some groups disempowered and disadvantaged. It misses that not everyone even has bootstraps to pull up. It also misses that not everyone has the same dream or ideas on what constitutes winning. The ideal may work for some but it is far from being a one stop solution.

Even more troubling for me, though, is the way it prioritizes sticking with the course over everything else. I fully appreciate the concept of perseverance and sticking with something through difficult times. Sometimes moments of difficulty are exactly what is needed to push a project to the next level. By pushing through the haze of difficulty, you level up to even bigger greatness. Sometimes the difficulty has nothing to do with the project and everything to do with the context of the situation. For example, as I write this I'm sitting at the end of what has already been a long, difficult, and extremely exhausting work week. I still have one more day until the weekend, and that day is filled with back to back staff and client meetings. The call of the couch and the temptation of chilled wine are tempting; however, I know they will still be there when I am done with this writing. I know this because I've been in this situation before. In fact, I am in some version of this situation nearly every time I sit down to do a free write. I also know that if I can push through that initial hesitation I will quickly enter an intuitive flow state and in an hour or so will have produced a solid draft that makes me happy, or at least one that I can live with. I also know that my commitment to this project is so important to me that if I give into the couch and wine temptation I will be more frustrated with myself tomorrow than if I force myself to write. I don't believe this type of situation, though, is the type that the irksome quitters never win phrase targets.

I believe "quitters never win, and winners never quit" falls into a category that I equate with toxic masculinity. It's along the same lines as the even more onerous saying that boys don't cry. To be successful you have to be tough, and to be tough you have to be hard. You push through all hurdles no matter what. If you are hurt, you suck it up and work through the pain. If you keep running into one obstacle after another, you keep running until you run out of obstacles. I've always wondered what the true underlying rationale is for this approach. Is it the Puritan work ethic that dictates you must prize work above all else and never leave a job unfinished. Is it part of the mythology saying that emotions and showing emotions are a sign of weakness? Maybe it's a part of the mindset that mandates you must be strong or at least appear strong in all forms. I guess in that sense, this could also be connected to the saying "never let them see you sweat."[64]

Why should we privilege being bull headed and sticking with someone who should be something that we know is not going to work? Is this another aspect of the importance of product over process? If so, why would we want to encourage half ass products over something that is better and more fully developed? The whole situation is puzzling and confusing and makes me want to quit.[65]

I believe that knowing when to quit is the thing that should be praised. Knowing when it is time to cut ties and walk away takes a lot of strength and ability. It requires you to admit and live into your vulnerability. This is the lesson we should be striving for and teaching. I think about the times I've been in the middle of a project what wasn't working and because of the power of the never quit

---

[64] Which in all honesty is just weird since sweating could be a sign of emotional distress but it's also commonly seen as a sign of physical exertion. Shouldn't it be desirable then to let them see you sweat as the sweat is a tangible physical marker of your strength and exertion.

[65] See what I did there?

ethos kept trying to push it forward. The entire situation keeps growing and growing in frustration. Let me use a specific example to help illustrate. One of the first larger canvases I worked on was a 36"x48" surface. I started it thinking it would be one of the manifestations of Green Tara. I had recently completed a smaller 24"x30" Tara and wanted to continue exploring her various manifestations. In the early phases of the process I found myself easily falling into a flow state. When coming to the canvas I would light a candle and bless the canvas with a misting of an essential oil blend. I keep a selection of these in my studio and would simply use whichever one I ended up grabbing for the day. I would then chant Green Tara's mantra "Om tare tutarre ture soha" 21 times, counting on my one of my malas. I would then put the mala on like a necklace and begin painting.

For the first Green Tara I was part of a virtual class. Over the course of 27 days, people around the world would work their own Green Tara within their personal studio. This process was so powerful and moving that I wanted to continue the energy by creating my own Tara painting process. In the early phases of the canvas I let myself play in whatever way came to mind in the moment. One layer was various words of compassion that I wanted to scribe onto the canvas. Another layer was an infusion of bright colors to symbolize freedom and childlike play. For another layer I soaked the canvas with water and flung paint at it so that the colors dripped and melted into each other. Another layer I painted dots all over the canvas with each representing a prayer for peace, joy, and love for all of my friends and family. I let this type of play unfold for several painting sessions.

Eventually I realized that a Tara image was emerging, and it was time to shift my focus so that I was more intentionally focused on her. I started building up her form by adding in colors and textures around the canvas. She began to take shape but every manifestation didn't feel right. I would work on her for a bit, get frustrated and walk away. I know this happens a lot with complex, big paintings so at first I didn't worry about it. I would put her aside for a bit and work on a different painting or play canvas. The next day I would return and try again until the feelings of frustration would begin to emerge. At some point I found myself dreading the return to her canvas. I tried to work on other canvases but I kept feeling the call of the Tara canvas, immediately followed by dread and frustration at the thought of trying to paint on it. A little while later I realized that it had been over a week since I had painted on any canvas. The dread and frustration of this Tara canvas was so strong that in avoiding it, I was depriving myself of a key activity that feeds my soul.

According to the philosophy of the quitters never win mindset, I should have sucked it up and pulled up my bootstraps and finished the painting. Who knows, maybe she would have eventually come out of the muck and mire of frustration. Instead, I quit the canvas. I stood in front of my easel staring at it and suddenly started digging through my supplies. I found my jar of gesso, grabbed a big brush and globbed two brushfuls of gesso onto the canvas. I grabbed another brush and using both hands started spreading gesso everywhere. As I worked I found myself smiling and feeling lighter than I had in weeks. I started chanting, "om tare tutare ture soha" and laughing after each soha. When the canvas was fully covered I stood back and sighed before grabbing an essential oil and blessing it with a misting.

Does that make me a quitter and by an extension a loser? For those people who buy into the ethos of the saying quitters never win, probably. Of course, those same people could probably also find many other things about my life that they would say make me a loser. Do I consider myself a quitter and a loser? Not even the tiniest bit. Since that time I've gessoed over a few more paintings that were causing dread and frustration. Knowing when to make the call to move into a new direction is tough, but it's also a sign of strength. It demonstrates that not only are you confident in yourself but that you trust yourself as well. Oh, and that Tara canvas now hangs in my living room as Lilith Who Speaks Truth to Power.

Meditation 10
Get Outside of Your Box

What are the boxes that keep you cycling around in a pattern of sameness?

I am in the midst of a moment of intense busyness, as opposed to the usual busyness that keeps me running around from one thing to the next.

I've been doing the legal advocacy work for a few months now, enough so that the files are beginning to accumulate. This work is on top of my usual work of being a professor coupled with the business I'm hoping to launch within the next year.[66] We are close to the end of the semester with the holidays looming nearer every day, so it feels like there is even less time in every day than usual. When I get in moments like this, I know that even though the work is flowing at this moment, it will soon ebb. Like the tide which flows in before ebbing out, work flows in and then ebbs out. To survive, I simply have to breathe deep, stick with it, and wait for that ebb moment to happen.

I've lived through these work ebb and flow moments for as long as I can remember. Learning how to handle these moments is one of those things that no one fully prepares you for in your adult life. I remember commenting one time in graduate school how I felt like I had so many different things needing to be done at once that I had no clue how I could get everything accomplished. One of my professors told me to wait until I was a professor, when I would long for the days when I could actually enjoy my semester breaks instead

---

[66] The side effects of those Renaissance Man dreams rear their heads again.

of using them to get caught up on all the work that gets pushed aside during the semester. I didn't respond out of respect, but in my mind I had lots of fun words for them. I was teaching three classes, the equivalent of a full time load, and one more class than they were teaching. I was also taking three classes with an average reading load of a book per week per class. I was conducting my own research to build my CV and for my dissertation project. Now that I'm a professor, I understand their comment more and long for the days when my work flow allowed time for me to read three books a week.

The ebb and flow of work in one sense is part of the human condition. To survive we have to ensure that our basic needs are met. We need shelter, clothes, food, and the other necessities of life. In order to provide for our basic needs, most of us need to work. Beyond these needs, however, we have emotional and spiritual needs of community and self-fulfillment. Trying to fit all of this into a 24 hour day presents a challenge. As a quick aside, the reality of the limited hours available in a day is one of the reasons I still sometimes play with the thought of being a Renaissance man. I want to be like DaVinci and only sleep four hours a day in small increments. I've often played around with the thought of training my body to do this and have dreamed about how much freedom and time it would create for me.[67]

When I find myself in a moment of too many things to do and not enough hours in the day to do them, I find myself easily slipping back into the confines, the boxes, that I learned as a young child. I learned early on that even if I could complete a task relatively easily and quickly, I shouldn't share this fact. Instead I should talk about all the work I put in and the struggles I overcame to complete it. I should take pride in how even though I had a lot of demands on my

---

[67] Of course, figuring out how to do this would require an investment of even more time.

time, I was able to juggle them all, even if I wasn't really successfully juggling them. I think in my younger years this was influenced by that working class ethos where there was a tangible pride in saying you worked for everything you got and that you never took handouts.[68] When I moved out of my working-class confines, I saw the same messages but in a slightly different form. In grad school, for example, there was a certain caché in bragging about how much effort you were putting into your research and how much time you spent preparing for class. I doubt that most people were spending the amounts of time they said they were, but there was still a lot of competition around the matter. There was one time when I was showing off some work I had done on a part of our website. I explained the process and said something about how relatively easy it was. The department chair pulled me aside later that day and sternly told me never to say something is easy to do. In the workplace, I am amazed at how I hear people talk about the things they do. I have worked on projects where I know exactly how much actual work each person has done. I'll sit in a meeting at a later date where they provide updates and be shocked at the ways they describe their work. The disconnect between what I hear and what I've seen is often vast.[69]

But at times, like now, when there really is a lot going on, we have to find ways to survive. This is where boxes come into play.[70] A lot of the stuff we have to do is repetitive on a regular schedule – making the bed, doing laundry, cleaning the house, taking out the trash, and all the other minutiae that consumes being an adult human living life. The easiest way to do these things is to create a routine. For example, every night before going to bed I empty out the coffee grounds from

---

[68] There is also a lot wrong and damaging about this ethos but that's a meditation for another time and place.

[69] I've been in a few meetings where the description of the work took longer than the doing of the work.

[70] I didn't forget the main point I teased way back in the opening of this meditation.

the morning coffee and grind more for the next morning. I load the dishwasher with any dirty dishes and hand wash any that aren't dishwasher safe. I wipe down the stove even if I haven't used it because in the morning the sun will shine on it in such a way that any dirt or dust still on it will seem magnified. Right before heading to bed I start the dishwasher if it is full. I do these things without much conscious thought, and the practice of them has become a type of pre-sleep meditation. The interesting thing is that despite this routine, most mornings I wake up convinced I forgot to start the dishwasher and am always pleasantly surprised when I walk into the kitchen and see that the cycle has run. I have several other routines like this both at home and work that allow me to complete necessary tasks without a lot of extra mental effort.

These types of routines are my boxes. I take comfort in knowing that what I need will be handled simply by stepping into the correct box. These boxes provide a momentary mental respite from the busyness of life while also allowing the work of life to get completed. In this sense the boxes are a positive and good thing to have in my life. However, the boxes can also have a more sinister or negative side. It is too easy to become locked into a box so that it shifts from being something that alleviates stress and mental exertion to something that operates as a command. If I let the box take control, then it begins to dictate my life. It also serves to limit other possibilities. For example, when I have family or friends over, spending time with them should take priority over cleaning or other commands of the box. It is easy, however, to forget this, especially when the box covers something important and necessary to daily life.

The box can also become a type of security blanket. Staying inside the box feels safe and secure so why move beyond the confines of it? For the boxes of daily life, using them as a security blanket is most likely not going to have any significant negative impacts. For example, the kitchen needs to be cleaned if I want to keep using it so if I follow the same pattern every day does it really matter? The box that kept me in my professor position, however, is a different kind of beast. The safety of this box is found in the security of a steady paycheck, benefits, and tenure protected position – all things that working class little girl learned are pivotal to life. Even though I knew I wanted and needed to do more, I convinced myself that staying was not only easier but better. Even though I was increasingly frustrated and depressed, I used the safety and security of the box as an excuse to stay long past the time I knew I should. I still have moments where those childhood messages about work lead me to question if stepping out of that box was the right decision.

Where the security of the boxes becomes even more pivotal, however, is when it comes to creativity. I have a few creative safety boxes I need to work to get outside of if I am going to continue to grow and expand as a Creative. I could approach every moment of creativity the same way and follow the same basic process. However, I know that when I allow myself to create intuitively and let the flow state arise, the end result will be wonderful. The key to achieving this is not to lapse into thinking that each step of the process needs to be the same, even if the end result will likely be amazing. In other words, I have to make sure I don't allow myself to get trapped in the box.

In addition, however, I desire to continue growing as a Creative. The usual ways I have for creating, whether it's writing or painting or creating something else, allow me to express myself and create things of beauty with deep insight. There is a sense of comfort in this. I know these approaches will work, so why change? There is also a certain expediency in these approaches. I already know they will work so I don't have to worry about devoting time to learning a new approach or way of creating. This is the trap of the box. It is only by getting outside of my box that I will continue to grow and expand as a Creative. I know this in my gut and my soul. My painting and writing practices are tangible pieces of evidence of this. Yet in times of extreme busyness like now it becomes easy to forget this. It is tempting to simply recreate the same things as a way of saving time and face. It is also a form of protection. To get outside my box and attempt something new or a new approach demands a vulnerability of self that I must accept. I must also accept that there is a learning curve that may take a while to master. I must acknowledge that this learning curve is part of the process and not reflective of me or my ability. Even in times where stress is flowing freely, if I allow myself to get outside of my box, amazing things will happen.

Meditation 11
Get Out of Your Own Way

What are the things you do that cause you to trip yourself up and stop moving forward?

I spend a lot of time talking about getting out of your own way even as I spend a lot of time getting in my own way. In other words, a textbook case of I need to practice what I preach.

I get in my own way in a lot of different forms but probably most often fall prey to overthinking. I am a master of taking the smallest thing and finding all the ways possible plus a few extra to turn it into a big thing that seems impossible to control. This habit probably started in grad school where I was only able to carve out tiny pockets of time to work on projects so I got into the habit of thinking about them regularly even if I didn't have time to sit down and work on them. One of the more interesting by products of this habit came in the form of dreaming my projects. When I was thinking too long on something I would often find myself dreaming the final product. When I woke and wrote down everything I remembered from the dream, I would find the project was in good from and often close to being done. I still have moments where I will dream paintings or essays.[71]

The most interesting and extended dream project came when I was working on one of the theoretical portions of my dissertation. I wanted to look at the ways we take up the multiple social and cultural

---

[71] Lilith Who Speaks Truth to Power, for example, wears a black panther necklace inspired by a pair of giant black panthers that kept appearing in my dreams while she was being created.

discourses that surround us and use them to create norms or expectations for how we are supposed to be. I was interested in not only how we talk about these things but also in how we actually change our behaviors to fit in accordingly. For example, why do many otherwise empowered women participate in harmful eating and exercise behaviors in order to try to fit into the unrealistic body dimensions that are determined to be ideal for feminine bodies?[72] For the theory section, I was working with bringing together the theoretical musings of Mikhail Bakhtin, Michele Foucault, and Kenneth Burke. Each of these scholars has a distinct look and identifying characteristics, and because I had immersed myself in their writings for a few years, I had their pictures seared into my memory. Somewhere during the writing process I started dreaming about the three of them discussing their works and the ways they overlapped as well as differed. This was interesting until the conversations turned into debates, strip debates. Whenever one of them would make a good point the other two would have to remove articles of clothing.[73] I still shudder when I think of those nights.

Back to my point, however – see how I got in my own way there with that distracting even if interesting, aside? I'm writing these meditations as part of NaNoWriMo. If you're not familiar with it, NaNoWriMo is National Novel Writing Month. People who participate accept the challenge to write 50,000 words, approximately 1,667 daily, during the month of November. I had always wanted to do it but November is a busy time in the school year as it is the countdown to the end of the fall semester.[74] Or maybe that was just the excuse I made to make myself feel better each year I let NaNoWriMo come and go without ever once sitting

---

[72] Even though I fully understand the damage in these behaviors, I can still fall prey to negative thoughts when I catch a glimpse of myself from an unflattering angle.

[73] Thankfully, I always woke up before the stripping progressed too far.

[74] This is yet another reminder of why now is a good time for me to leave higher education.

down to write. This year on October 30, on a whim that may have involved a couple glasses of wine, I created a NaNoWriMo profile. I knew I didn't want to write a novel, and at this moment still don't. However, I also knew I had a book inside me that was calling to be released. To keep myself accountable to myself and the process, I told a few close friends who I knew wouldn't nag me but would gently nudge me to keep going.[75]

In my usual writing process I spend a lot of up front time thinking through the general content and trajectory of what I'm going to write. I compile my sources and any original research I may use. I generate a general outline or plan of the project. I collect a couple yellow legal pads, a selection of black gel ink pens with a few other colors for editing. I find a special journal that I will dedicate to the project and use to track any thoughts or asides that happen during the writing process. I love the ritual of this part of the writing process as it creates a way for me to honor the entire process and acknowledge its importance. Once I start writing I will find a spot, either at home or in a coffee shop, and will usually write in quick 30 minutes bursts of free writing. I try to do three to four of these in each sitting. When I finish a section of writing, I will type it up. The act of typing serves as a first edit as I am able to add more content and refine the writing in place. The whole process served me well over the years, until it didn't. Until I found myself getting in my own way.

A passion project I have been thinking about and preparing for my entire career, even though I didn't consciously realize it, was what I call Compassionate Conflict. I have never been one of those women who avoid conflict and actually enjoy engaging in a rousing debate every now and then. I realize now as an adult that my approach to

---

[75] I think I secretly hoped at least one of them would discourage me so I could use them as a scapegoat for skipping NaNoWriMo again.

conflict is grounded in the ways my childhood friends and I would interact in our daily activities. We would regularly stage debates and evaluate each other on who made the better arguments.[76] It wasn't until I was well into my 20s that I realized many people go out of their way to avoid conflict.

I believe that conflict is a necessary part of our humanness. Conflict is what allows us to grow and expand and advance as a society. If it weren't for the conflicts engendered by feminist activists, I probably wouldn't enjoy the professional status I have today.[77] I don't, however, believe that the ways we usually approach conflict are good or productive. Too often conflict is approached as something to win, making the interaction combative and frustrating. My goal with Compassionate Conflict is to shift the understanding of conflict from a combative interaction to an act of peace by incorporating mindfulness practices into it. The manuscript for the Compassionate Conflict project is one I have been thinking about for over a decade and actively working on for a couple years. This is how I found myself getting in my own way. As I got into the editing phase, I realized the stuff I really wanted to talk about was the mindfulness practices. While I like talking about the basic conflict stuff, it wasn't as enjoyable, but still necessary. I kept reading and reading the parts I liked, working on perfecting them, even though I don't believe in perfection. Every time I would venture back to the conflict stuff I would get frustrated and give up before finishing. The whole project currently sits on my dining room table taunting me in its incompleteness.

One of my goals with taking the NaNoWriMo challenge, then, was to get out of my own way and approach my writing differently. Even

---

[76] This is also why I probably found myself joining and enjoying the debate team in high school. It also likely factored into my first career choice of attorney.
[77] I definitely wouldn't have been able to have credit cards or a mortgage in my own name.

though I knew I didn't want to write a novel I still didn't know what I did want to write. I knew I had a lot of random thoughts in my head about creativity and the creative process that needed to come out. I also knew I had a lot of thoughts on the reality of shifting my professional trajectory from Professor to Creative. I didn't, however, know how or even if these thoughts were connected. I decided my approach for the month would be to change up my writing process. In order to more easily track the daily word count goal, I decided I would write directly on my laptop. One of the reasons I usually avoid this, beyond the fact I like writing by hand, is because the automatic editing functions of most writing programs are counterproductive to my creativity. However, I knew that the best way to stay true to the word count was to use the laptop. I decided I would sit down each day with no plan other than a thought or prompt and simply write until I had at least 1,667 words.

I also committed to not reading anything I write until the month is over. I am writing this in the second week and am battling for the third day in a row my desire to go back and read some of the things I've written. I feel this constant urge or tug dragging me toward the master document where I paste each day's writings. When I sit down to read in the chair by the table where I keep my laptop, I find myself glancingly lovingly at the computer and thinking maybe I should just open the document and scan the format, knowing that I will catch some words and phrases along the way. I also know myself well enough to know that if I do this I will mostly likely fall into the temptation of reading the entire document. I also know that it really doesn't matter. It's not like there are NaNoWriMo police who are going to arrest me for not sticking true to the process, a process I designed for myself. I could read the whole damn thing and no one would be the wiser unless I told them. However, if I give into this temptation, I am likely to end up getting back in my own way. No matter what I say to myself I will feel the urge to start editing. I will start obsessing about word choice and wondering if I should supplement my words with the words of another expert. Perhaps most damaging, however, is I will lose whatever flow this is that is keeping me churning out those 1,667+ words per day. While I still might finish the project, it will be a different project. It will be a product that might very well be good, or it might be a manuscript that sits on my dining room table, taunting me. Instead I will, for once, practice what I preach and continue living into this intuitive flow state and wait another 19 days before diving in and reading.[78]

---

[78] But I still feel that pull to read it all.

Meditation 12
Fake It 'Til You Make It

What are the things you stop yourself from doing because
you don't think you are capable of doing them?

I don't know when I first heard "fake it 'til you make it," but I'm pretty sure that I laughed it off. I can confidently say that I didn't dream how much it would become a mantra for so many different parts of my life.

Before I get too far along, I feel the need to acknowledge that I am well aware of my qualifications and skills and all the things I bring to the table. I have lots of letters after my name and years of experience. I have a CV that runs well over 20 pages long. Even when I struggle with not having the exact credentials requested, I admit that I have a vast toolbox of miscellany that help qualify, and often over-qualify, me for the things I seek to do. I am also conscious of the fact that questioning my ability to do things is a distinct enactment of privilege granted to those who have enough time to ponder life and the way it happens.

Despite my qualifications and skills and things I bring to the table, I find that on most days I still struggle with an intense sense of impostor syndrome. More often than not, if I'm being honest with myself, I feel like I'm still faking it. The situation presents a weird yet interesting juxtaposition in my life. My public persona can be described in many ways but perhaps loud and proud is the most descriptive. I am a vocal advocate for the causes I believe in and the people I care about.[79] I speak truth to power and believe that doing so is part of my obligation as a caring human. I'm not afraid of taking a public position on controversial issues even when faced with vehement and loud opposition. I will not back down from a public stance even when I am threatened or shamed into doing so. Nearly everything I do involves some aspect of public presentation, and I like public speaking even though I define myself as an introvert. For all intents and purposes I appear confident in all that I do. Most days, however, this confidence is a mask I don to cover the insecurity I feel.

It's an interesting situation to be convinced that you aren't qualified to do the thing you've been asked or hired to do. I have tangible proof that I am qualified by virtue of the fact that I'm here doing the thing. Yet for whatever reason I still feel that lingering sense of being an impostor. I'm convinced someone will figure out that the whole situation was a mistake and pull the proverbial rug out from under my feet. Despite the fact I have no evidence this is likely to happen, the thought persists. A perfect example of this is my tenured faculty position. This is my seventeenth year on this campus, and I earned tenure several years ago, so it would take something significant for me to be fired. I know this intellectually. However, I still worry that I don't really belong or that the administration will decide I'm not really doing the job I should or some other irrational act will occur that will show I'm not worthy. What is especially interesting about these thoughts is that on several occasions over the years I have taken up battles with various administrators. Even in pushing back, I wasn't asked to leave so why should I be worried about it now?[80] That's the thing with impostor syndrome – it doesn't make sense or reside in the field of rationality. It creeps in and buries itself deep

---

[79] My momma bear side is always ready to jump into action.
[80] And since I already know I am exiting on my own terms, why should I care?

inside your psyche, planting roots that go ever deeper. Like tentacles, they grab onto anything they can.

Another interesting aspect of my impostor syndrome is that I have reflected on it and understand the nuances of why it appears. For me, a big part of my impostor syndrome rests back in that working class background of mine. During my formative years I was surrounded by messages that your worth as an individual is directly connected to your work, and that work was hard. Even if your work wasn't physical labor, it was something you did in a place for at least 40 hours a week and that you mostly hated doing. Part of this message was that office jobs, defined by their white collars, weren't "real work." The people who did these jobs didn't understand "real work" and had it easy in life. As I'm typing that I can see all of the social biases wrapped up in these thoughts, as well as the insecurities such thoughts hide. Understanding that phenomenon doesn't change its impact, however. Not only do I now have one of those white collar jobs, but I have one that even many people holding traditional white collar positions don't understand. To the masses, being a professor means you only work a few hours a week while you are in the classroom, and even that isn't real work because all you are doing is pontificating on useless theoretical minutiae that no one really needs to know to live a good life.[81] I spent a good portion of my career making extra work for myself because of the intensity of these myths and the ways I had internalized them. I felt it important to demonstrate that even if I was faking it, I was working hard and putting in all the long hours.

As damaging as the mythologies of work are, however, probably the biggest part of my impostor syndrome rests in the fact I am a first generation college graduate. I didn't grow up dreaming about going

---

[81] There are many other misunderstandings and myths about being a professor but that's another book for another time.

to college and never really thought it was a possibility for me until my high school academic advisor told me I should think about college. Even though I knew I was a good student and took classes with students who were planning on going to college, it never crossed my mind that the college path could be one for me as well. This is also the time when those roots of impostor syndrome started taking hold.

Impostor syndrome isn't a label that is given to you but one that you adopt voluntarily. My little high school self had never heard of it, yet the roots were already being planted. These roots take hold in the recesses of your solitude. Even when you don't nurture them they grow and multiply. I think of them like a snake coiled up in silence just waiting for the right moment to strike. I am fascinated by how no one needs to ever call you an impostor or say you don't belong or even question your being there in order for the impact to be felt. Even being aware of the existence of impostor syndrome and how it plays out in your way of being in the world doesn't change this impact. Just because you are aware of it doesn't mean it doesn't happen.

This whole meditation was prompted by the appearance of impostor syndrome earlier today. An interesting possible professional career shift came onto my radar in the last couple days. While I love teaching and my students, I have known for a while that my passion for it as a profession is waning. There are many factors contributing to this, but I've come to accept that this part of my journey is nearing its end. I've thought about possible new directions but nothing solid has developed. The opportunities that have crossed my path, while tempting have not been tempting enough to make the switch. This one, though, is different. I have returned to the position description multiple times, and each time find more about it that makes me excited. I asked a friend about it this morning and learned there is an internal candidate. This information immediately caused a change of heart. My only thought was, "Oh, if there is already someone in line who could do this position, there is no way I would be considered so I shouldn't spend the time applying." When I look at what I just wrote, I can laugh at myself. I can also see all the flaws in my logic. That's the thing with impostor syndrome, it defies all common sense and logic. It exists in its own little world of power and prestige, creeping in when you least expect it.[82]

And here I am, nearing the end of this meditation and I haven't even begun to write about the ways impostor syndrome impacts my creative self. I feel like that exclusion in itself is yet another manifestation of the syndrome. I could have written this whole meditation with a focus on creativity and with examples of how impostor syndromes appears in my creative life. I didn't choose that route, however, because there's still that part of me that is hesitant to accept the label of Creative. I didn't give voice to this fear until just now. I worried that any of the examples from my creative journey wouldn't be as powerful as the ones I chose to feature in here. Afterall, I can back these examples up with all those degrees and letters after my name. What do I have to back up the examples from my creative life? A bunch of paints and brushes and works in progress? Look at the ways that even as I'm writing about impostor syndrome that little fucker finds a way to worm its way in – who says that degrees are more important than the tools of my creativity? Why am I letting this random, hypothetical person dictate this to me? And all of that is a perfect example of the power of impostor syndrome. Even after I have spent all this time unpacking its dimensions and thinking about it and acknowledging it, it still finds a way to make its power known. The roots of my impostor syndrome seem to have found a home deep in my psyche. Maybe that is the lesson I need to learn today – I can't control the impostor syndrome; I can only

---

[82] I ended up not applying for the position but not for any of the original reasons. I decided that my time was better spent building up my own business so that I have more time to devote to creative pursuits.

control myself. The best thing I can do is tell impostor syndrome to fuck off.

Meditation 13
Take a Leap of Faith

*What do you need to stop thinking about
doing and just leap in and do it?*

Sometimes you need to stop thinking and start doing. The key is figuring how to take that first jump.

"She took a leap of faith and grew her wings on the way down." I have a bracelet with this saying on it. The bracelet is one of my favorites even when it isn't in current rotation. As fate will do, however, it jumped onto my radar this morning. I have a good selection of fun and inspiration jewelry, and on one of my dressers I have a bowl with random bracelets in it.[83] Even though I haven't touched that bowl in months, for some reason today the brown leather band that supports the metal plate with the saying on it was calling to me.

I think one of the reasons I am drawn to the sentiment of this saying is that it reminds me to keep moving forward. It encourages me to have faith in myself, even when I don't. Plus I love the image it evokes. I picture a woman tentatively standing on the side of a cliff with, of course, a beautiful expanse of rocks and trees behind her. She looks behind her. She glances up at the blue sky, enjoying the bountiful white clouds. She looks in front of her and down to the rocky expanse at her feet. She closes her eyes and takes a deep breath, enjoying the scent of the air. She opens her eyes, stands tall, and leaps into the air. At first she begins to fall, quickly moving toward the

---

[83] I also have many wonderful friends who feed my love of meaningful accessories.

rocks below her until a shuffling noise fills the air as she rises above the cliff edge and soars off into the clouds, leaving a trail of rainbows in her wake.[84]

What I find interesting about this bracelet coming onto my radar today is that another set of wings, abandoned wings, also reappeared on my radar. The abandoned wings are one of the paintings in progress currently taking up residence in my living room. I don't know exactly how long they have been in their current spot other than they've been there all this year. It's now mid-November so the math is pretty simple. Before I get too distracted I think it will help to understand how the wings in process came to be.

After I painted that first Buddha I started fully diving into painting and creating all the time. In a sense, I guess I was waking up each day and taking leaps of faith. I didn't have any plans for all the paintings and other things I was creating. I simply knew that I had to create. I woke every day with a compulsion to grab a paint brush and make something. All those years of putting creativity on the back burner until my "work" was done must have left those creative juices ready to rush out. The Buddha painting came about from an online self-directed class I took. The process of the class was enjoyable, and I appreciated the ways we were encouraged to not feel constrained by simply recreating what we saw in the videos. When I completed the class, I knew I wanted to take more.

For a few months, I lived into my good student way of being and signed up for all sorts of online painting classes. I scoured Youtube for painting videos. I was a proverbial sponge, looking for any creative options I could find. I also used this time to begin testing out various art supplies. I've always loved having options. Whether it's things such as purses or shoes or journals or places to work and

---

[84] Damn, now I need to paint this scene.

create, I like to have a variety of them to switch back and forth between. Finding a love of painting, therefore, gave me a whole new set of tools and supplies with many, many options to choose amongst. I found myself quickly becoming particular about which brushes and paints and substrates were acceptable. I laugh when I think about how this whole creative journey started on a whim where I knew nothing about the difference between craft paint from the dollar store and Golden acrylics. In only a matter of months, however, I was lusting over hand crafted watercolor paints and debating the merits of natural hair versus synthetic brushes.

My path during this part of my journey was unknown, a never-ending series of leaps of faiths. Every morning I would wake up and not know where I would end up but have faith it would be someplace amazing. One morning I found myself reading an email about an upcoming nine-month long creativity and coaching training. I had seen information about this training when taking the Buddha class and thought it was interesting. I dismissed it then telling myself I didn't have the time or money to invest in it. This time, however, something clicked differently. Even though the time and money investment were the same, I paused. The more I thought about it, the more I found myself getting excited about it. During lockdown when I hadn't spent as much money as usual, I had been able to save a little sum of money for the first time in my professional life.[85] Technically I had the funds available, and I can always find a little bit more time in my schedule to add in things that are important to me. I left the e-mail open and went to teach my class.

I found myself still thinking about the training during class when students were working in small groups. On a whim I decided to text a couple close friends about this random thing I was thinking of

---

[85] Another myth of the life of professors is that we get paid lots of money. Maybe a few superstars do, but most of us make less than our students will earn within five years of their graduation.

doing. I expected they would remind me how busy I already am and gently suggest adding more sleep to my schedule if I was going to add anything. Almost instantly they both texted back that they loved this for me and were excited to see me do it. What? How could this be? I put it all out of my head and went back to teaching. On the way back to my office I stopped into my friend's office to tell him about my random thought, readily expecting he would be the one to put me straight. His response was, "Oh, my god. This is perfect for you. You so need to do this. I have never seen you this excited or glowing like that before." What the holy hell kind of bizarro world had I wondered into? More importantly, why couldn't I accept that maybe my friends knew me better than I knew myself?

By the time I got back to my office, I decided to trust their words since I couldn't trust my own in this moment. I clicked on the registration link, completed the form, put in my credit card information, and clicked submit. I anticipated I would feel instant buyers' remorse. Instead I felt giddy. I think I might have even giggled. I printed out the recommended supply list and started art supply shopping.

Once the training actually started I enjoyed it, after we completed our initial Zoom meeting that is. I was extremely nervous for that meeting and kept waiting for someone to call me out and say I wasn't in the right place.[86] The training was a good way for me to continue expanding my skill set while also learning to trust my creative gut more. I found myself surrounded with a cohort of wonderful women, many of whom have become friends. I still had moments where I didn't feel worthy, but I also found myself enjoying the process.

---

[86] Impostor syndrome rears its head at the least opportune times.

The second phase of the training involved a longer series of sessions that blended meditative explorations of self with painting. The final painting for this session was a set of wings to represent our flying on to creative freedom or something like that. I came into the session not really being excited about painting wings. I don't even know why I had such a bad attitude about it, but it persisted. I saw others in my cohort posting pictures of their wings paintings in progress and reminiscing about how moving the process was and how much they were loving it. I kept trying to get to that point but couldn't find it. I kept pushing forward and eventually rough painted in an outline of a set of wings. Still not happy with it, I started adding color. I found myself avoiding the painting and putting other canvases in front of it on the easel.

The wings stayed on my easel for a few more weeks before I finally moved them in their unfinished state to a pile of other canvases in progress. Every so often I would look at them and think about finishing them, but it never happened. Eventually they moved from the studio to the living room and found a resting spot against the wall at the bottom of the stairs. I pass by them daily without really registering their presence. However, today they found a way to jump into my consciousness.

I have a friend who is in the process of opening her own hair salon in the next couple of months. We met yesterday to update my hair color[87] and to talk about some of the logistics of her new place. I must have been thinking about it when I came downstairs and saw the wings. I thought to myself that hanging them in the studio for the grand opening could create a wonderful photo op for the event and help boost her social media presence. I then started thinking about how maybe we could do a mini exhibition of my other paintings. I've been thinking about starting a series of colorful

---

[87] This month's choice is platinum with a purple underlayer

abstracts that would go wonderfully with the aesthetic she is planning for the interior.

Even though she and I had never discussed any of this, I was already moving forward with the plans in my head. I basically planned a whole new series and exhibition without once asking her opinion. The interesting thing is I didn't have any pushback for myself or criticism or any of that other negative self-talk. I think I took a massive leap of faith and expect to start growing those wings soon. In the meanwhile, I believe it's also time to return to the wings painting and finish it as well.

Meditation 14
Put Yourself Out There

What are some ways you can put yourself
out in the world more?

We live within the circles of energy we create. To do this, however, we have to take chances and share ourselves and our work with others.

Much of the creative process involves overcoming your personally created limitations, whether they are in the form of the inner critic, the unfounded fears, or any of the other ways we get in our own way. I know that being a Creative is something I not only want to do but that I need to do. It is a key part of me. If I don't create every day, I feel off, as if something is missing not only in my life, but from me. It may sound trite and cliché, but creating is my life blood, the thing that feeds my soul and makes me a better person.

An important part of the creative process is putting yourself out there in the form of your work. If you want to make a living out of your creating, this is clearly something you must do. However, I would argue that even if you only create for yourself putting your work out there is still important. I think of the act of sharing your creative work as part of a karmic cycle of creating. It is part of the energy that surrounds us and into which we all add. Everything that we do creates energy, and we can decide what kind of energy we want to generate. There are those individuals who seem to thrive on creating and recreating negative energy; those folks who spend an inordinate amount of time complaining or instigating drama. The ones who are able to take any situation and find something bad about it. Even when they are able to afford and do things that many others can only dream of, they will find a negative twist to their lives. I always feels sorry for these people even as I try to limit my interactions with them.[88]

I believe it is much more productive and enjoyable to focus on creating and recreating positive energy. We experience what we produce, so if we put out positive energy we will get positive energy back. I think it's important to note that when I talk about positive energy, I am not thinking about or advocating for toxic positivity where the focus is only on things that are positive and the negative are ignored or left unacknowledged. It's important to understand and accept that bad things happen. Some days you are in a funk and don't want to be around people. Sometimes horrible things happen in life, even to the best people. We can acknowledge these things and push through them without letting them weigh us down or become an obsession. In fact, I would argue that the negative things are a pivotal part of appreciating the positive as they help us gain and remember perspective.

When we create, we have the opportunity to create more of this positive energy. When I paint words of joy and compassion on my canvas, I am sending thoughts of joy and compassion out into the universe. The process of inscribing them onto the canvas generates an energetic vibration that ripples out for all to enjoy. When I play with color, splashing and flinging it at the canvas, I always end up smiling and laughing at the process. I think of this process as my painting dance of joy. My brush jumps from paint to canvas to water and back multiple times. I move around the studio and often move the canvas around the easel. I grab my water bottle and mist the

---

[88] I used to work with a woman who always had a story about how much her situation was worse than that of anyone else. I always wondered what happened in her life that caused her to feel the need to always be the biggest victim in the group.

canvas with a blessing of water which then blends with the paint to create ripples of colorful joy that wend their way down and around the canvas. Everything that I add to the canvas raises the karmic vibrational energy of it, and this energy ripples out into the universe.

Creating the canvas is the first part of the cycle of creating. It is possible to also be the last part. I don't ever have to do anything with my canvases. They can stay lined up in my studio forever, or until I decide to repurpose them into something else. However, I feel that this inherently limits their possibility of reaching their full potential. When I put myself out there by sharing my creations, their vibrational energy is then expanded. The power of that joy and compassion embraces all who come into contact with them. The smile and laughter of my paint slinging encompass all who see the remnants of it on the canvas. The power of their energy transfers to those who see them who in turn spread some of that energy within their own circles of influence. I like to think of it as ever expanding waves of happiness working their way into the lives of random people.[89]

I've been thinking about these things today because of a random request that came across my email. I should confess that I don't always practice what I preach. As much as I am singing the praises of putting yourself out there in this meditation, I have only sparsely been putting my own work out there recently. I have lots of ready excuses that I could trot out to explain this inaction, but I'm just going to own it as a moment of personal weakness that will pass soon. In the past, however, I have put myself out there. I've created designs that have become greeting cards for friends and family. I have gifted paintings to various important people in my life. Probably the most common way I have put myself out there, though,

---

[89] Maybe a representation of this idea is something that should/could become a future painting.

is by posting pictures on social media where the masses can see them. The first time I posted a picture of a canvas I struggled for a long time to build up the nerve to do so. All of those insecurities and worries my inner critic is good at creating came flooding into my mind. The fear of being called out as an impostor was immobilizing. The worry that I would be judged and evaluated as not worthy[90] was overwhelming. It took me over a week to finally build up the nerve to take the dive into creating a post. Now, I don't even remember what that first post was, but I do remember that there was not even one negative response. I know that I shouldn't have been surprised by this, but yet I was. Of course I also know that I shouldn't have struggled with making the post, but like I said, I don't always practice what I preach.

Since that initial post I have created hundreds of posts. Before I fell into this most recent cycle of not posting, I went through a phase of posting daily creative meditations. These were either pictures of my morning watercolor practice, when I still had one or snippets from works in progress that prompted an interesting meditation to begin the day.[91] What I found when I put myself out there by putting my art out there was that I felt more energized. It was as if every time someone looked at my work, they were sending me some of their energy in a type of perpetual energy feedback loop. The other surprising and fascinating thing was the actual feedback people gave me. Even though not everyone interacted with my posts in terms of comments or likes, I began to realize that many of them were not only looking at the posts but also looking forward to them. I heard on many occasions from someone who I had no idea even looked at my posts how much they enjoyed them. That little working class girl

---

[90] Worthy of what I don't know as that was never part of the equation
[91] And now that I've written that, I believe it is time to get past this recent funk and return to daily creative meditation posts..

afraid to embrace her creative side part of me still has a difficult time accepting this, but I'm working on it.

Back to the random request. A work colleague of mine, and coincidentally one of those people who I didn't realize interacted with my work, emailed me asking about some mini paintings that I had posted a few months ago. She wasn't exactly sure what they were but remembered they were some sort of winter scene with pine trees. After some back and forth we figured out they were mini paintings I had created for holiday cards. The only reason I even remembered these paintings is because I kept one and have it posted on my refrigerator. These were the first paintings I turned into greeting cards and sent out to people during lockdown. It seems fitting that these would be the paintings that would remind me of the importance of putting myself out there. The request is that she would like to use them as the design for a postcard mailing she is preparing. We still haven't finalized the logistics of the situation, but the request reminded me of why I need to keep pushing forward and not isolating myself. The request also makes me feel honored. Even if we aren't able to make my design work for the mailing[92], it is amazing to have been asked. I don't mean that in the compulsory also ran way of saying I'm honored. I am genuinely honored that she not only remembered my work but also thought enough of it to think that it deserved to part of her mailing.

I'm feeling the need to end this with a pithy yet motivational pitch, which is probably more for myself than anyone else. Here goes – go commit to putting yourself out there and generate more creative karmic energy. We need more positivity in our lives and the world, and we can never have enough color and energy mixed with a touch of joy and compassion.

---

[92] She ended up not being able to get funding for the project.

Meditation 15
Have Fun and Play

When was the last time you did something just for fun?

Have fun and play!" I don't know why this command came to me but this morning during my ease into the day morning routine I found myself thinking on the concept.

As we mature into adulthood, play becomes one of those things that get pushed to the backburner or buried in the basement of our memories. This makes sense as adulthood brings with it all the responsibilities of adulting – paying bills, cleaning everything, all the steps of food preparation[93] followed by more cleaning, family life, and all the other minutiae that fill our days. Time for play, unless of course it's play with your children or other littles in your life, becomes less of a priority. In addition, play seems to be one of those things that carry a tinge of stigma when you're an adult. Think about the last time you heard someone talking about playing just for the sake of playing and without making an excuse for it or qualifying the play time with talk of all the work they did before and after. While I understand how play oozes out of our life, I also mourn its loss.

When I affirmatively started my journey into embracing creativity, taking moments to play were pivotal. I feel that creativity demands an attitude of play. You have to be willing to experiment and try new things, and if you have fun while doing it that's even better. My best creations are those where I have allowed myself to have fun and not

---

[93] Just the amount of time and energy demanded by all the steps of feeding yourself – buying, processing, cooking, eating, cleaning – is a whole helluva lot.

worry about anything. This isn't to say that I have always mastered this process. I still find myself struggling at times with maintaining an attitude of play throughout all the phases of my painting and writing.

One of my current works in process is a Goddess of Compassion painting. I love all things goddess and have devoted hundreds of hours to reading goddess stories. I have a half sleeve tattoo on my arm of the goddess Persephone emerging from the depths of hell. Every room in my house features at least one representation of a goddess, and my living room hosts two different goddess altars. It's not surprising, then that my art often features goddess imagery and symbolism. The Goddess of Compassion painting came about on a day when I was struggling to feel compassion for a colleague who was being especially difficult. I found myself fuming and angry and unable to shake these feelings even after meditating for thirty minutes. Inspiration struck, and I decided to create compassion for myself, my colleague, and the situation by channeling compassionate energy into a painting. I grabbed a canvas and started playing.

I began by painting the word compassion over and over on the canvas until I began to feel some of the negative energy leave my body. I then started adding colorful symbols and glazes. In less than an hour my attitude had shifted, and I focused on playing with color instead of the frustrating colleague.[94] Eventually it came time to paint the form of the goddess on the canvas. I grabbed my brush, poured some white paint onto my palette, and helped her emerge. In the process I realized that one of the symbols I had painted on the canvas looked like her necklace, one of those happy accident moments of painting. I only had a few minutes left to paint before having to get ready for a meeting, so I grabbed my Nickel Azo Gold

---

[94] I wish I would have found this outlet for stress relief earlier in my life.

tube of paint, one of my favorite colors to work with, and did a light glaze over her.

The next day I returned to the studio excited to work more on the Goddess of Compassion. I was eager to feel the joy and happiness working on her yesterday had generated. Instead, however, I found myself frozen while staring at her. The next obvious steps would be to begin refining her features and fine tuning the overall design. I decided to work with Quinacridone magenta, another one of my favorite colors. Every time I approached the canvas with my brush I felt it being repelled away. Part of my intuitive painting process is trusting my intuition even when it seems counterintuitive to what I want to do. I have had many occasions now where this same kind of repelling feeling happens. I embrace these moments as ones in which the canvas is helping me understand what it wants to be. I think of these moments as ways that the canvas helps me get out of my own way. I didn't think much about the moment and moved on to another painting in progress who didn't reject my attempt to add some magenta to it.

That was a few months ago now, and like my wings painting and many others, the Goddess of Compassion remains unfinished. Every time I tried to return to her, no matter what I did I couldn't return to that feeling of fun and play. Even before I started writing these meditations on creativity, I had been reflecting on all the ways I am still hesitant or reluctant to live fully into my creative life.[95] I could probably write a whole separate book about just those issues, but for now I only want to focus on the tension between wanting to enjoy those play moments and feeling the need to be a serious adult. In part I know this goes back to that childhood baggage about your worth being connected to your work. Therefore, play, even creative

---

[95] I finally had to admit that part of my hesitancy was connected to how fully living into my creative life means making that change in my professional life.

play, needs to have its rightful place. Even as I write those words, I cringe at the severity and rigidity of them. One of my many goals with writing these meditations on creativity is to take my embodiment of my own creativity to the next level, and if it helps a few other people along the way that is a wonderful added bonus.

When the command to have fun and play appeared this morning I decided to heed the call. Thankfully, fate was looking out for me as I found myself with an extra 20 minutes before I had to leave the house. As I thought about what I could or should do, I wandered into the kitchen and spotted my watercolor station. Again, fate had my back as it was only a couple days ago I was thinking that I really should break it down and reclaim the counter space. Now, the watercolors were calling me to play and create. I decided to return to the practice for which I had created the station and do a four-minute watercolor meditation.

I first began daily four-minute watercolor meditations as a way to change up my morning routine. In my "your worth is determined by your work mindset," I used to wake up in the morning and right away dive into work. I charged my phone by my bed[96], so I could easily grab it and start checking e-mails while heading downstairs. Yes, walking down stairs while checking e-mails is not an ideal way to start the day or ensure your safety, especially when you have a Diva Dog who wakes up ready to play and who likes to weave in between your feet when you walk. Despite its questionable safety, this practice served me well for a long time, until it didn't. I believe that the way you start the day has a strong impact on how the day plays out. If you begin with the energy of work and stress and deadlines and all those things that come with e-mails, then that is the energy that you will take into the rest of your day. My thought, therefore, was to shift this energy by shifting my morning practice.

---

[96] I no longer do this. I don't even bring my phone into the bedroom now.

Instead of starting with busy energy, I would begin my days with creative energy, hoping that creativity would then infuse everything else I did as my day unfolded.

The shift began by not taking my phone upstairs with me at night and instead leaving it to charge in the kitchen. I would come downstairs, let the Diva Dog out, and start heating water on the stove for coffee. I would fill the French press with coffee grounds and let Diva Dog back inside. By this time the water would be ready to be poured over the coffee grounds. During the four minutes that the coffee was steeping, I would turn to my watercolor station and paint, playing around and enjoying the swirls of color and shapes. By establishing the watercolor station in the kitchen, I had no excuse not to paint. I love coffee, so that four minutes of wait time was going to be there anyway. I found that within only a couple days, the watercolor meditation practice was already a habit. Even on those days when I would wake up tired or cranky and swear I wasn't going to paint today, by the time I was pouring the water into the French press I was looking forward to the first splash of paint on the page. I continued this practice for months, filling several watercolor journals with fun and interesting bursts of colors. For a while, I would take my morning meditations and add doodles to them so I could end the day with creative energy as well.

My four minute watercolor meditation today involved me painting strings of coils across the page, working from one corner up to the opposite corner on the top. I used a different color for each coil and simply let my brush determine which watercolor pan it wanted to visit. I didn't worry about composition or color saturation or any other technical aspects of painting and instead simply enjoyed the play of color on paper. It shouldn't come as a surprise to know that the energy created in that moment is still coursing through me. I am glad I heeded the call and have decided it is time to bring back watercolor meditations daily. I'm even thinking about grabbing my pen after dinner and adding some doodles to the coils as an evening wind down. The best bonus, though? We are currently getting a ton of snow as part of a winter storm, so I will be working from home tomorrow, and I have already pulled out the Goddess of Compassion painting and plan on having fun and playing her into completion.

Meditation 16
Trust Your Gut

What are the things you tend to second guess yourself on?

Stop second guessing yourself and trust your gut. This is one of the many things that I preach better than I practice. It's a work in progress much like all those canvases leaning up against the walls in my living room.

I think I have a pretty good gut, when I listen to it. One of my super powers is the ability to come into a situation and see it from multiple perspectives. For the longest time, I thought everyone had this ability. It was only after I was well into my adulthood that I realized the ways I see the world and the things happening around me differ from others. Integral to this super power is that when I trust my gut, I can usually figure out the best solution to any conflict or problems that arise. But, there's that issue of second guessing myself.

The practice of second guessing appeared on my radar today during my morning routine. Whenever possible I like to ease into my day. Most mornings that means drinking coffee and spending time with Diva Dog while reading the paper. Over the last few years I've also become hooked on doing various brain training activities. Even though everything I do in my professional life requires lots of mental flexibility and fast processing, I have an irrational fear of decrease in cognitive processing or memory loss as I age. I know it's irrational and have no family history of dementia or Alzheimer's, yet here we are. My current rotation of training includes refreshing my French language skills, a daily mixed blend of language and math problems, a refresher of basic math skills[97], and a daily word game. These are in addition to the random challenges I will create for myself. Past challenge highlights have included crocheting a different motif every day for 30 days, drawing a mandala a day for 30 days, and the 30 day[98] daily personal essay challenge, which I have done multiple times and in multiple formats. I am always at my most competitive when I am competing with myself and have yet to meet a personal challenge I won't eagerly accept.

Today's reminder of why I still need to practice second guessing myself occurred during the daily word game challenge. The focus of this game is to guess the five letter word in six tries. After each guess you are notified which letters are correct as well as which are in the proper place. My standard first guess is the word "teach" which today yielded the "t" in the correct spot with the "e" and the "h" being correct letters in the wrong spots. Immediately, my first thought was the word "there." Instead of trusting my gut, though, for some reason I dismissed it and instead tried the word "theme." You can probably guess what happened next – theme was wrong and there was correct. The interesting thing is that this isn't even the first time I've done this exact same thing with this game. You would think by now I would have learned to stop second guessing myself and instead trust my gut. Apparently, this is a lesson which I must be hit over the head with several times before I fully internalize it.

I've thought a lot about where my second guessing, or when I'm being less generous not trusting myself, comes from. Like any human, I have many examples in my past of times I made the wrong choice and suffered the consequences. There was the time as an

---

[97] Even though that Engineering major didn't pan out, I still have an affection for math. I like to think of the juxtaposition of my love of reading and creating and doing math problems as an example of my moving closer to embodying that Renaissance Man ideal.
[98] Clearly I like challenges involving the number 30.

inquisitive child I wondered if staplers work on tongues. The painful answer is yes. There are the multitude of bad romantic partners I was convinced were going to be the love of my life. There was that moment when I thought I could be an engineering major followed by the thought of being a political science major followed by the fleeting thought of being an elementary education major. There is also that brief space when I was a practicing lawyer, which is especially interesting now 20 years later when I am tiptoeing back into the practice of law. All of these examples, as well as the myriad others from my past represent moments on the path of my life where I made a choice, a wrong choice, but the right one in the moment. These types of things are not the same as the second guessing choices.

When I second guess myself, I am ultimately saying I don't trust myself. Even though I know in my gut what I should do, for whatever reason I override that thought. I think a lot of things factor into this process. There's the ever-present impostor syndrome which keeps me thinking I don't belong or have the qualifications to do what I'm doing. Even when I am over qualified and have experience in whatever the thing is, that little impostor syndrome voice finds a way to creep in. With second guessing myself, though, I think an even bigger contributing factor is the fear of making the wrong choice and then being forced to grapple with whatever consequences ensue from there. It sounds silly when I put it down in words, but the feelings are real. It sounds especially silly when you think about my second guessing myself on the word game – what horrible consequences would ensue from going with my gut? Who would even know that I took this move unless I chose to tell them?

That's the thing about second guessing yourself, though, it's not about being rational but instead about the irrational fear engendered by insecurity. When I don't trust my gut and second guess my choice, I am letting my insecurity override everything else. My qualifications, skills, experience, and everything else I bring to the table evaporate into mere nothings. In a very real sense, the act of second guessing and not trusting your gut is another form of immobilizing behavior – when I do this I am stopping myself from acting.[99] This becomes especially cumbersome and detrimental when it happens in the space of creating.

Second guessing myself in the creative process occurs in various different ways. I just started to write a sentence and then after five words, deleted them out. I could call this editing, but in a first draft do I really need to focus on editing? If I were to practice what I preach, every single thought and word would be included. I teach this process as word vomiting and encourage my audiences to vomit out every single thing without worrying about if it makes sense or forms complete sentences or anything else. With painting, I find myself doing a similar thing when I will add a burst of color to the canvas and instantly question it. The painting version of computer keyboard deleting is grabbing a wet cloth or baby wipe and eliminating the offensive swipe of color. What would happen if instead of second guessing myself in those moments, I left the offensive color or wrong words as part of the composition? I wonder how many things of glory I have backspaced and baby wiped out of existence?

Even more troublesome than these minor acts of second guessing myself, though, are the larger moments where I have allowed myself to second guess myself into complete immobility and abandonment. I think of all of the paintings in progress around my studio and living room. I think of the thousands of words memorialized in journals and files around my office without doing anything to make that happen. Every time I return to an abandoned project I wonder, why

---

[99] I keep learning more and more about why it has taken me so long to move into my creativity.

did I stop? What did I think was so wrong with this work that I abandoned it? The tentacles of insecurity run deep. Even when I find these abandoned projects, I don't do anything with them. I let them continue to reside in the journal I move to the bottom of the pile so I can pretend it doesn't exist. I move the abandoned painting into the living room and put it behind its peers. Instead of embracing these works as things filled with possibility, I put on my blinders of insecurity and pretend they don't exist.

Here's the thing about insecurities like this – once you acknowledge them and call them out for what they are, it becomes difficult to continue to let them control you. This is what happened when I first allowed myself to ponder that question of what my life would look like if I let myself embrace my creativity. I was forced to think about the years I spent dreaming about being a Creative without doing anything to make it happen. Instead of trusting my gut, I hid behind my profession.

Having written this meditation, I know that my choice to step away from my profession is an affirmative act of trusting my gut. If I can trust my gut for a big step like that, can I really continue wearing the blinders of insecurity and pretend all these abandoned projects aren't screaming out for completion? I could if I wanted to continue deceiving myself and not trusting myself. However, in writing these meditations I've come to realize that one of the many goals I have for them is to make myself more accountable to myself. To celebrate the awesomeness that I know I embody even when I question it and myself. Perhaps most importantly, though, is my hope that by letting myself think and write about the various dimensions of creativity, my creativity, I will find my way back into my own creative practices. The whole time I've been writing this, two abandoned projects have been floating around in the back of my head – a book and a larger painting. I am publicly declaring that within the next week I will pull both of these projects out of their hiding places and return to them.

I will see them through to completion even if I never publish the book or publicize the painting. As I am working on seeing them through to completion I will stop myself from second guessing and trust my gut so I can let their glory live into existence.

Meditation 17
Impermanence and Letting Go

What do you continue to hang onto because you are afraid to let it go?

I'm not a hoarder in the sense of living in a house filled with items I am unable or unwilling to let go of. I do, however, have a tendency to save things, sometimes for longer than I should.

I know that in part my insistence on saving things is connected to my fear of not having them. It is grounded in those times of life when I was barely living paycheck to paycheck . Many weeks, the only thing saving me was my willingness to take a chance that I could write a check on a Wednesday night and that it wouldn't be cashed and processed before I could deposit my paycheck on Friday. These were the days when I would "borrow" toilet paper from work so that I wouldn't have to go without at home. The times when I would go the gas station and carefully pump exactly $2.34 gas for which I could pay with the change I scavenged from the couch cushions. It's easy to look back on those times through the rosy lens of nostalgia, but they were tough. At the same time, however, I wouldn't go back and change them because they have become a pivotal component of who I am today, how I walk through the world, and why I privilege giving my time and money to those who are in the midst of difficult times.

Those days are well past me now, and I have plenty of toilet paper at any given time. I still viscerally carry the weight of those times, though, in the ways I connect with certain things. While I laugh about borrowing toilet paper now, the shame of that moment continues to linger in my soul and resonate with my way of being. One of the things I regularly buy at Costco are the multi-packs of

Charmin extra soft toilet paper. Buying Charmin feels still like an indulgence and buying 24 rolls at a time is simply decadence gone wild. However, I find that when I get down to that last package of six rolls, I begin to worry about what will happen if I run out of toilet paper. I won't, of course, and I know this fear is irrational, but even irrational fears feel real. Part of this fear resides in the thought that while I am safe and financially stable now, there is still that little voice warning me that it could all be taken away at any time. I've come to realize that this also feeds into my hesitancy to shift the focus of my professional life. Irrational fears run deep.

I've been thinking about letting go today because my morning started at the shelter with a staff meeting where we said goodbye to three colleagues who are moving on to different adventures. We spent time going around the room and for each individual telling them how much we appreciated them and how they have impacted our time together. The meeting was filled with laughter, memories, and of course some tears. Saying goodbye is always hard, but it's just that tad bit harder when you not only enjoy the people you work with but like them as well. At this point in my professional career, I've said goodbye to many colleagues and in some ways am used to it. However, being used to it doesn't make it any easier. Moments like these remind us of the impermanence of life.

We know that the important people in our life could die at any moment, and we are often reminded to tell our loved ones how much we love them.[100] What we don't tend to think about, however, are the other important people in our life. It's just as important to tell them why they matter. This seems like one of those super easy, well duh things to say, but sometimes the easiest things are the first ones forgotten or neglected. Expressing care and compassion

---

[100] If you haven't told your special people you love them today, stop reading for a moment and go do so. Even better, take a moment to write them a card or letter that they can return to in the future.

verbally like this is also something that isn't regularly practiced or promoted so it can feel weird at first. I remember the first couple times I told a group of people I love you all so much. I cringed inside expecting to be mocked or laughed at. I'm happy to report that neither of those things happened, and now I regularly toss "I love you" into my interactions with people important to my life.

Practicing impermanence and letting go and embracing them is essential to creativity. For me, the first level of accepting impermanence harkens back to the lingering effects of those paycheck to paycheck days. I've mentioned my love of art supplies, but in case you missed the point, I love buying art supplies. Whenever I'm in any store, and I see paints or pens or tablets I instantly gravitate to them. I have to remind myself that unless this is a brand new product, I probably don't need it, and even then I most likely still don't need it. While I love buying art supplies, however, I don't always love using them, or to be more accurate using them up. I love the process of creating and exploring new ways to blend different materials together to create new textures. For example, I am currently obsessed with splashing acrylic inks on top of acrylic paint layers. The viscosity of the ink is much thinner than the paint so they tend to move and flow over the paint layers in interesting ways. They pool in spots where there is a build up of acrylic paint while gliding over smoother areas.[101] But buried deep inside is that fear that because I couldn't afford art supplies during the lean days of my life, I need to ration the ones I have now and hold onto them. I want to put them in a cabinet and keep them, just in case. Once again irrational fear makes an appearance. I know that I should use the supplies because they won't stay stable forever. Just because I keep them doesn't mean I will be able to use them.[102]

---

[101] Just writing that makes me want to stop writing and go play with ink.
[102] I do the same thing with journals.

The other way I see impermanence creeping into my creative process is the fear of letting something go. In both my writing and my creating, I think this fear is part of the reason I get stuck on not completing some of those works in progress. I've been thinking about this in terms of the Compassionate Conflict manuscript whose notes and pages still reside on the corner of my dining room table. I spent over a decade thinking through conflict and why it's necessary. I then spent a good few years refining my approach to teaching others about alternative ways to approach conflict. Finally I dedicated over three years of research and writing to the manuscript, the manuscript that isn't quite finished and which needs serious editing. I've already done what I consider surface editing – refining content and working on structure. During that process, I realized that my approach to the material was still more academic than I wanted it to be. Therefore, a significant overhaul is needed, including removing big sections that I thought were ready to go. Even though I know this is needed, and I know the end result will be amazing, the manuscript continues to gather dust on the corner of my dining room table.

The manuscript is only words. They are words that I combined where before there was nothing. They are words that are saved in a computer document so getting rid of them doesn't even mean permanently deleting them. I can easily cut them from the manuscript and put them into a new document so I still have them. I also know that my ability to combine words in interesting ways is not going to go away. Even if I do accidentally delete something I can always rewrite it. I have many examples of times when this has happened, and the rewritten version is nearly identical to the deleted version. A similar thing happens with my paintings. I will have a color pattern that I love or a design sequence that makes me happy. It doesn't really work with the overall painting, however, and needs to be modified. It's only paint on canvas, and I have a lot of paint and a lot of canvases. I can always recreate the color pattern or design sequence. Like my writing, I have tangible examples of times when I have done this. Writing and painting are creative processes that don't expire or magically disappear.

I know all of this. Yet, that irrational fear that I will somehow ruin what I have done continues to control the moment. It's like I somehow took a vow of permanence to these particular words in this particular configuration and worry that if I break that vow something horrible will happen. Like I said, it doesn't make rational sense even as it continues to keep me in its grip. During those paycheck to paycheck days, there were many times I was forced to give up, in other words sell, something that was important to me. I needed the money more than the thing, so I would make the tough decision to sell the thing. To help process and accept these moments I would remind myself that I didn't have the thing ten years ago, and if it was meant to be with me, it will find its way across my path again. I didn't have the language of impermanence and letting go at that time, but now I can see that was exactly what I was practicing. Many of those things, or similar versions of them, did find their way back to my path.

I think the lesson I need to take away from this meditation is more than simply a reminder to embrace impermanence by letting go. This is an important part of the lesson. I should adopt a revised version of my old mantra – I didn't paint or write this ten years ago, and if it was meant to be I will write or paint it again. I think the larger lesson I am meant to take from this meditation is that I am no longer that person who was afraid of her creativity and that my creativity is a permanent part of me. It's not going anywhere I don't go.

Meditation 18
Shut Up!

What are some of the ways you need to tell your
screaming inner critic to shut up?

Sometimes the only way to practice self-compassion is to tell
yourself, your inner voice, that it's time to shut up.

I am a firm believer in the need to practice self-compassion and be
gentle with yourself, even if I don't always practice this in my own
life. It is easy to lapse into believing the voice of my inner critic and
jumping on the bandwagon of negative sentiments. I understand that
part of this is a self-protection response. If I say all the bad things
about myself or my work or whatever the focus is, then no one else
can say them and hurt me. Speaking the negative sentiments creates
a type of emotional break wall or buffer of protection. The obvious
problem here, however, is that it can become too easy to start
believing the negative sentiments such that you limit yourself or
otherwise hinder your advancement. For example, as I'm writing this
I can hear this running dialogue happening in my head – not that
word, why would you say that, is this really something that other
people care about? I'm used to this background noise when I write,
so I try to drown it out. This isn't to say that I'm always successful,
though.

At times, this inner voice can change from a constant hum to
something closer to a scream. I know that in busy times, when I am
pulled in multiple directions at the same time and my stress level
creeps up, I am more susceptible to the screaming critic. In these
situations, I am tired and emotionally vulnerable, so it's tempting to

fall prey to the negativity. Likewise, when I am working on creating something for someone else or for public display or presentation, the hums are replaced by screams. In these situations, that scream is trying to protect me from the potential harsh criticisms of others, even when I don't need such protection. In a sense, this inner screaming critic is kind of a bully. It creeps in when I am weak or at my most vulnerable and attempts to take control. At these times, I have two options. I can fall prey to the screaming critic and be a victim, or I can tell it to shut up.

I'm thinking about this now because of an incident that happened a few nights ago. I didn't realize how much it bothered me until I found myself dwelling on it again. The moment happened mid-evening after I had eaten dinner, done a final check of e-mail, and was thinking about the rest of the night. All throughout the day I had told myself that after dinner I was going to paint. I have a few 36" x 48"[103] canvases in progress and wanted to set up a station in the living room on the floor so I could add some fun play elements to them. I had been thinking about next steps for both of the canvases and woke up in the morning having dreamed about both of them. I was excited to get working on the next steps of these paintings, yet I couldn't find the energy to get up and move. We have recently been experiencing our first cold snap, and I was snuggled in my reading chair under my super soft skull blanket and with the Diva Dog cuddled up next to me.[104] I decided to practice what I preach by being gentle with myself. I told myself I could read a couple chapters while my food digested and then paint.

I love reading and could easily spend the entire day stuck inside a book, and in fact I have had glorious days where that is all I have

---

[103] I have a thing for big canvases even though I don't necessarily have the wall space to accommodate them.
[104] I could blame the dog, saying I didn't want to disturb her, but that would just be a lie.

done. One of the worst tortures for me is when I am so sick that I can't concentrate enough to read. It's horrible. I also know, however, that I can use my love of reading as a crutch or shield of avoidance. When I have something I don't want to do, it is all too easy to hide behind a book and use the act of reading as my tool of procrastination. Afterall, reading is still doing something and it's doing something of value unlike something trivial like watching television.[105] I can be quite persuasive and snobby simultaneously. I can easily convince myself that it's not an issue of me avoiding doing the other thing, it's merely a matter of me allocating my time to this specific endeavor in this moment. This evening became one of those moments. A couple chapters turned into a few chapters which morphed into some more. I was reading the book on my Kindle with the function telling me how many minutes are left in the chapter turned on. I started another chapter that would take me five minutes to finish. I then gave myself a little pep talk about how if I set up my painting station by the couch I could still snuggle under the skull blanket.

If you love reading like I do, the Kindle time function is the most enabling tool ever created. It is too easy to play an endless game of one more chapter when you have a solid estimate of exactly how long that one more chapter will be. For advanced players, those who are seriously obsessed to reading, Kindle also has an indicator of how much time is left in the entire book. I have had many nights where I have completely skipped over the one more chapter game and simply gone straight to the one more book version of it. This night, I finished my five minute chapter and made the mistake of checking how much time was left in the book – 63 minutes, barely more than an hour. I closed the Kindle, telling myself that no, I was going to paint. Then the dog moved and sat up, placing her head on my chest

---

[105] No shade on watching tv – I end most nights by indulging in cringe worthy reality shows.

so she could look me in the eyes. I am a sucker for puppy eyes.[106] Plus it was that moment right before the furnace is ready to kick on for its next cycle, so the house feels even colder than usual, making the coziness under the skull blanket extra enticing. It doesn't take a lot to figure out what happened – I reopened the Kindle and finished the book.

When I finished the book, and downloaded the next one in the series, I thought about what I would need to do to set up the painting station. I also thought about how tired I was. I checked the time and realized it was going on 10:00, and while I usually don't go to bed until around midnight, it probably wasn't the best idea to get wrapped up in another endeavor where I would be likely to lose track of time. I had an early start the next morning with a full day of meetings. I took a pet the puppy break to think about it and decided that the best thing to do would be to pour a glass of wine and find something mindless on television so I could decompress before bed. Within seconds of making the decision that bullying mean critical screaming version of Peggy appeared. I found myself rhetorically beating myself up for not painting yet again and spiraling down into a pit of negativity.

I sat with these thoughts and feelings for a moment. I believe it's important to honor your feelings, even those that are less than pleasant. It's equally important, however, to not get caught up in the quagmire of negativity they can generate. In the past it was all too easy for me to get caught up in this mess which then would generate a self-perpetuating cycle of inactivity and negativity. This night, I told myself to shut up. I actually spoke the words out loud, scaring the dog from her cozy cuddle nap. I had never told myself to shut up before, and if I'm being honest I felt a mix of emotions about it. I was surprised at the vehemence of my words at the same time I was

---

[106] I'm still not blaming her. I totally own my actions.

taken aback at them. I rarely use the phrase "shut up" and can't remember the last time I spoke it, let alone saying it to myself.

On the surface, it seems like telling myself to shut up is completely antithetical to my message of practicing self-compassion. Shut up seems like a negative response to a negative sentiment. In this instance, though, I think it was the best response. We are nearing the end of the semester, so I exert a lot of energy on the emotion labor of helping my students manage the stress of classes. That day I had taught two classes and met with ten different students individually to answer questions or reassure them that they could do the work they were convinced they could not. I had taken a quick trip to the grocery store to restock essential food items and wine. I had spoken with three different clients in various stages of either obtaining or enforcing a Protective Order against their abuser. I had done a load of laundry and some basic house cleaning work. I'm sure there were other miscellaneous chores and errands I had done but forgotten about as well. The point is that I had already had a full day at a time in the year when there was a lot of extra things happening. At a time like this, choosing to read over doing something else doesn't have to be or shouldn't be a negative choice. It is should be simply a choice that is right in the moment. Being gentle with myself, therefore, means allowing myself to admit my limitations as a human and spend an evening cuddled under the skull blanket cozied up with the Diva Dog reading all the one more chapters to the end of the book. Being gentle with myself, therefore, also means telling myself to shut up.

Good Enough

What does "good enough" look like to you?

Just like it's important to know when to quit, it's equally important to know when your efforts are good enough. Figuring out when this is, however, can be difficult.

As part of my personal challenge in writing these meditations, I come into each day without any idea of what today's meditation will be. During my morning meditation I think about the fact that at some point later in the day I will write a meditation and open myself to seeing what is revealed to me throughout the day. This doesn't require any change in my daily routine other than paying closer attention to those little things that arise. Once I realize what the prompt for the day will be, it seems like I then see it popping up all over my life.[107]

Today's prompt jumped to my attention this morning. We are in the early days of winter; however, Mother Nature has decided to show off and has been dumping snow on us all week. In the last two days, we have received just over eleven inches of the stuff. To add insult to this injury, less than two weeks ago, temperatures were in the 70s, and I was still wearing sandals. I live in the Midwest, so I should be used to these types of drastic weather shifts by now, but they always take me by surprise. It started snowing late yesterday afternoon and continued overnight. I woke up to the latest pile up – six inches to

---

[107] Does this mean I'm manifesting it to happen or am I just seeing differently? Hmmmm…...

be exact. This means that in addition to my morning meditation and coffee drinking/puppy cuddling time I would need to fit in a winter wonderland workout, aka shoveling.

The first snowfall of the winter is glorious. The trees, recently naked after showing off all of their colors, hold mounds of snow in creative groupings. The lawn looks like a big white fluffy blanket. When the sun shines just right, there are glistening crystals of light everywhere. Pulling out the shovels and putting them to use isn't necessarily fun, but it is a good way to use muscles that haven't been used that way since last winter. Even the Diva Dog gets into the joy of the first snow and races around the yard at full speed on the trails I shovel out for her.[108] That first snow was last week. This morning's snow represents the third snowfall this season already.

I live on a corner lot, meaning I have a lot of sidewalks that need to be shoveled. A few years ago the city improved the sidewalks on the sidewalk making them wider so more people can more easily walk on them. To help put this into perspective, they are now wide enough that I can drive my car up to the front door on them and still have room on either side to walk next to the car. I also live on a street that is a fairly popular connector street with a steady stream of traffic. The good news about this is that it is always one of the first streets plowed. The bad news about this is that those plows create piles of deep slush at the end of my driveway. In other words, shoveling snow, especially six plus inches of snow is a good size endeavor. It's kind of like an extra workout within the workout.

This morning I decided to indulge in a cup of coffee and puppy cuddles before venturing out to start the process. Part of this was pure procrastination on my part, but part of it was practical since the

---

[108] Yes, she is a very well loved dog with lots of attention. She's also a smaller dog, so if there's more than a couple inches of snow her belly ends up caked in tiny little snow balls unless I create paths for her.

feels like temperature was -4°F. After an hour, and a temperature rise to feels like 0°F, I ventured out. Whereas the first shoveling expedition of the year is fun and a reminder of those underused muscles, by the time the third one comes around, it's just work. I put on my adulting pants, however, and I dug in. As expected, the end of the driveway was filled with over ten inches of heavy, gray slush. The piles on either side of the driveway, leftover from the last shoveling workout, already stood at three feet tall. I knew, therefore, that in addition to shoveling the snow I would need to walk it to a different area to dump it. This extra shoveling activity adds an element of balance trying to keep the snow on the shovel and one of agility in trying to keep myself from falling on the slick surface to the regular cardio and strength portions of the workout.

After the first two passes of the driveway trying to get to the car, I was already feeling my muscles singing. In part, this is because to get to the driveway, I had to shovel my way down the sidewalk for a good forty feet, so the driveway passes came after this. I kept working away, telling myself that my reward would be some fun painting play in the afternoon. Once I was able to get a path around the car I took a shoveling break to clean off the piles of snow amassed on the car itself. Although, when there's this much snow at once, cleaning the car isn't so much a shoveling break as it is shoveling with a snow brush instead of a shovel. Five minutes into this process, I realized it would take several passes and that I would have to reshovel the paths I had just shoveled. This was the moment when I looked around and first thought "good enough, I just have to do it good enough."

Usually when I shovel, I don't obsess about getting all of the areas completely down to the concrete.[109] As long as the areas are generally cleared, some lingering areas with coverage are fine. With the wide

---

[109] Not cement

sidewalk, unless we only have an inch or two, I don't fret about doing the entire thing and try to get about half the width shoveled. Even with these concessions, the entire process is quite the endeavor. Today, however, I looked around and realized that there was no way I was physically or mentally up to doing all of that. I kept working on clearing the car and thinking about "good enough" and what would good enough look like today.

Knowing what good enough looks like and when it's ok to say this is a moment where I am only going to do what's good enough is an important act of discernment. The inquiry requires you to not only understand but accept your limitations. It demands that you be gentle with yourself and accept that your best in this moment might not be what you had hoped, but that's still fine. I think of these moments of accepting good enough as practices in vulnerability and strength. You have to allow yourself to be vulnerable to the limitations of yourself at the same time you have to be strong enough to accept those limitations and move on.

I still struggle with the acceptance of good enough in all of my creative endeavors. I know that at least part of the cause of all those unfinished manuscripts and momentarily abandoned canvases is my inability to say this is good enough. This is also another one of those things I am much better at preaching than practicing. I work with writers all the time and remind them that everyone gets edited. Editing is an important process that helps make our writing even better than it was.[110] It is important not to let yourself get trapped into a cycle of perpetual editing where you are trying to reach the unicorn of the perfect of sentence or word or manuscript. Instead, the goal should be to the do the best writing you can at this moment, knowing that it can be edited later, by you or by an outside reader.

---

[110] I also admit that editing is the hard work of writing.

In painting, the process is similar. I don't strive to create photo-realistic paintings. I like abstract art and whimsical images; however, I have moments where I get caught up in whether the thing I am painting looks like it should. Does that paintbrush look like a paintbrush or some weird stick thing? Does her nose have the right shading or does it just look dirty? Worries like these take me out of the meditative flow and change the way I interact with the work. Instead of being a moment of meditation and fun, the focus shifts to a chore that must be completed. When I allow this shift to happen, it becomes easy to abandon the project as it is too mentally draining to continue trying to make it happen. If however, I could remember to find the "good enough" spot then, even in the moment of questioning the brushiness of the paintbrush, I can find my way back into meditative flow.

I don't know that I have the answer for how to make that shift happen, other than to accept like everything else that is part of the human condition, it is something that gets easier with practice. I'm hoping that I can remember my driveway moment of today. Once I got the car cleaned up and the paths around the car shoveled once again, I decided that instead of doing the full two car width of the driveway I was only going to do enough for my car. It's supposed to warm up into the 40s later in the week, so the rest of the snow will likely melt before the full driveway gets called into use. This also meant that I didn't have to do the extra balance and agility portion of the workout. For the sidewalks, I decided a path of one shovel width was going to have be enough. It's wide enough for one person to walk down without having to take any extraordinary measures to stay on cleared concrete. All of this would have to be good enough.

Oh, but I did end up doing lots of running paths in the backyard for the fur baby. A Diva Dog's interests always need to be considered and honored, even in the spirit of good enough.[111]

---

[111] Ha! As soon I hit period after that sentence, I said, "that's good enough for now."

Meditation 20
This Too Shall Pass

In what ways should you be more patient with yourself?

Some days the only thing you can do is breathe deep, count to 10, and keep doing that as many times as it takes to find your reserve stores of patience.

I have not always been a patient person, and perhaps I still am not one. I know that since I started meditating and creating and living into those aspects of myself that light my passion instead of simply being chained to the idea of work,[112] I have more resources to navigate through those moments where patience is the only way to manage. That is not to say that I always act in a patient manner or don't end up getting frustrated. I'm human and a work in progress, so I have flaws, many flaws.

As I went through my day today, I found my ability to practice patience being tested time and again. I don't know that I necessarily mastered each moment, but I made it through the day without yelling at anyone so I'm calling that a win.[113] Through my meditation practice, I've come to realize more about myself. Even though I don't currently have a regular self-reflection practice, I find that going through life with the presence generated by meditation allows spontaneous self-reflection to happen. While describing my day to a friend late this afternoon, I realized that upon reflection the entire

---

[112] And to the demands of a challenging job.
[113] A friend gifted me a lapel pin that says, "Didn't stab anyone today." Some days this truth hits close to home.

day was one that helped me find areas where I still need work in the patience category.

The first lesson in patience happened this morning in my class. This week is Thanksgiving week, so it's a short week of classes. For this particular class it was also the last class where we were covering new material. I designed the class session to be one where collectively we would reflect on the semester to date and prepare to shift to final projects and assignments. I also know that during short weeks like this, many students choose to start the holiday early by taking off the entire week.[114]

I went into class mentally prepared to see a few missing faces and to see extreme fatigue on those faces present. I was not prepared, however, to see half the class missing. I gave my standard lecture about how much I appreciated that the people present came to class and how missing the class before a break is a bad choice. Professors remember these things when it comes time to write letters of recommendation. While speaking I could feel myself getting angry that so many students had decided to skip this meeting. I had to pause and take a deep breath, plus a drink of coffee, and remind myself to calm down and be patient. I had to remind myself that this too shall pass. I wasn't angry with the students who were present, and I wasn't even angry with those missing students either. The crux of my anger was with myself and all of the things I could have done differently to ensure they made a different choice, even though I know that isn't possible either. They are adults, and I'm not their parent and therefore not responsible for the choices they make. My lack of patience was more directly connected to the way the choice to skip class reflects a lack of respect for my time, time that I could

---

[114] It took many years of teaching and meditation to get to the point where I can accept that choice even though it's not a choice I would make or one that I agree with.

have devoted to painting or reading or just drinking coffee and cuddling with the Diva Dog.[115]

My next lesson in patience happened in the afternoon when I was in court. No matter how many times I go to court, I still get nervous and antsy in anticipation of a court hearing. [116] I know these feelings are a combination of me taking my clients' cases seriously coupled with the vestiges of that ever present impostor syndrome. Today I also came into the courthouse experiencing a lot of frustration. This client is one that doesn't listen very well and often does the exact thing I've said not to do. For this particular hearing, they went against my advice and filed their own paperwork despite the fact I had said that doing so would trigger a defensive attack from the opposing party. We were in court today because that is exactly what happened. Adding to my frustration was the fact that the client had never provided me the evidence they said supported their matter, so I was walking into the situation completely unprepared. As if all of that isn't enough, the client arrived over 30 minutes later than we had agreed to so I spent all that time hanging out in the courthouse lobby making random small talk with the police officers on duty.

My first test of patience was during that time waiting. As the meeting time came and went, I felt anger creeping up and trying to take over. I sat down, took a deep breath, and reminded myself that in just a couple hours this would all be done. I made a couple jokes with the officer about how no one told me in law school how much of my lawyer life would be spent hanging around the courthouse rotunda. I waited and walked around and waited more, so much waiting. I reminded myself to be patient and that the situation was beyond my control. When I finally saw my client coming up the stairs I grabbed

---

[115] It has only been since admitting that I am leaving higher education that I've been able to admit that these moments feel like acts of disrespect.

[116] When I was a newly minted lawyer, I would vomit on mornings I had to be in court. Only feeling anxiety and nerves are a significant sign of progress.

my briefcase and went to greet them. Upon reflection, I can see how this moment of patience testing was another manifestation of someone disrespecting my time. Instead of being present in the moment and practicing patience, I started thinking about all of those other things I could be doing. In this particular situation, my anxiety about going into court made it easy to slip from mindful presence to distracted impatience.

The appearance of the client also fed into the next test of patience. Not only does this client have a habit of acting directly counter to my advice, which tests my patience in more ways than I ever imagined, but they also tend not to fully listen to me and interrupt me when I am trying to explain things. I absolutely hate this behavior on so many levels. The interruption is rude, but it also disrupts my train of thought causing a distraction. Intellectually, I know that interruptions like this are reactive forms of communication often done as a form of defense; however, that doesn't make them any easier to handle when they happen. Today the client appeared with a posse of supporters so there were many others waiting to interrupt away as well. I reminded myself to breathe, be patient, and establish boundaries about not interrupting.

What's interesting is that before today and writing about the testing of my patience, I didn't see how this test of my patience is connected to the wasting my time test of patience. With the interruption test, what I am feeling in response is the disrespect inherent in the rudeness of interrupting. The interrupting itself is frustrating, but what I am really reacting to is the way I feel I am being (mis)treated. Both of these situations test my patience not necessarily because of the specifics of the situation but because of the larger emotional baggage of disrespect. The more I understand that my impatience is really about establishing respect, the easier it is to handle it in the future.

Understanding my need for patience in moments like those I confronted today not only helps me to better engage with others and maintain the calm presence I prefer, it also helps me better engage with my creativity. When I think about the moments in my creative practices where I feel impatience creeping in, they also tend to fall into categories. For example, yesterday I was adding a detail to one of my larger canvases. I was working with a beautiful alizarian crimson that I had thinned down with some glazing medium. I wanted to add a section of vining curlicues but I didn't want them to overpower the surrounding areas of the painting. The glazing medium essentially waters down the pigments in the paint so you see a less intense color on the canvas. It also thins down the paint and can make it a runny consistency if you use a lot. When I started painting the curlicues, I realized they would take longer to dry than I had anticipated. In other words I needed to sit and be patient. As with today's tests of patience, I first felt myself moving toward anger. This was the only full free day I had, and I had hoped to do a lot of work on this painting. Instead I was stymied in how much I could do. In this sense, I think this creative impatience is another manifestation of the disrespect of time from today. My time, which is limited and valuable, was not being used the way I intended. Unlike today, however, this moment was completely of my own doing.

The other way I see impatience creep into my creative endeavors is when I am trying to do something that isn't working out. When I'm trying to get my thoughts out in an essay, and nothing on the page makes any sense. When I'm trying to remember the exact word that is needed in this sentence, and my vocabulary decides to take a vacation. When I'm trying to paint a figure, and it ends up looking like a messy glob on the canvas. In all of these situations, my impatience is caused by my own perceived incapacity, my inability to do what I want to do in that particular moment. This is similar to my impatience caused by interrupting where I'm not able to speak as I want in that moment. The big difference, however, is this moment is caused by my own actions.

In moments like this, I need to remind myself to be patient with myself. If I can practice patience with others in my life, I should be able to do the same with myself. Instead of getting angry I should have taken a deep breath and create.

Meditation 21
Take Your Time

*Where are places in your life you can
slow down and be more present?*

Some days I need to remind myself to slow down, be present, and enjoy the things happening around me.

A few years ago I was invited to give a keynote lecture at a health and wellness conference and another one a few weeks later at a women's empowerment retreat. These two events were some of the key moments that moved me deeper into the study and practice of mindfulness.[117] In talking with the planners of each event, we explored various topics that might be of interest to those in attendance. Up to this point much of my research had focused on how women's lived experiences of body shape and demands on ideal feminine beauty influenced the ways they communicate with each other and with themselves.[118] I was beginning to shift my focus, though, into various aspects of incorporating contemplative practices into our daily communication practices. On a whim I suggested that I could talk about our obsession with busyness, even though I had nothing specific in mind. Both conferences were intrigued with whatever BS I strung together, and I ended up creating a talk entitled "I'm too busy to be well."

---

[117] And upon reflection, they were also some of the first inklings of the beginning of the end of my traditional academic life.

[118] I'm still fascinated by this topic and always ready to riff on it.

Without going into all of the specific details, my main point was that while most everyone agrees that spiritual, mental, and physical wellness is important, actually making and taking time to incorporate such practices into our daily lives doesn't always happen. I believe there are many reasons wellness practices get pushed to the side, but perhaps the biggest contributing factor is our cultural obsession with busyness. There is a certain cultural caché to being busy, such that busyness becomes a type of badge of honor. At least once a day I run into someone and ask how they are doing and am told how busy they are, "Busy, busy, busy."

It's important to acknowledge that there are situations where busyness is not an option. I think about the single parent who is working to support a family while raising that family as well or individuals who are forced to work two or three jobs in order to make enough money to pay their bills and string together some sort of life. These situations are a different beast from the badge of honor busyness. In these situations, being busy is a necessary condition of life. In the others, being busy and talking about being busy is a way of showing importance. There are lots of practical and psychological reasons why this type of busyness occurs, but my interest is in how it works against those wellness practices that are in our better interests.

When you run around being busy all the time, the act of being busy becomes both shield and a sword. As a shield, it protects you from having to think too deeply about anything or engage too much with other individuals. It provides a way for you to be physically present without being fully mentally present. As a sword, being busy helps you carve out of your life things that are trivial or unimportant, or that you like to think are trivial. In a culture where capitalism and consumption are prized, those things that aren't connected to making or spending money often tend to be devalued and looked down upon. I have lost track of how many times when I mention my daily meditation practice someone makes a dismissive comment such as, "Oh, I don't have time for all that woo woo touchy feely kind of stuff, but I'm glad you do."[119] So much condescension and passive aggressiveness packed into a few simple words.

What I find especially interesting about this busyness phenomenon is that doing things like daily meditations are not only good for you but they actually carve out more time in your day. It seems counter-intuitive but ever since I started meditating on a regular basis, I find myself being able to accomplish more in a given day. I am confident that if it weren't for the focus and clarity of vision that meditation provides, I would not be able to maintain regular painting and writing practices on top of all my professional responsibilities. Even though I don't get paid for meditating, it pays off in many other ways. Taking the time to meditate and simply be in the moment creates more time for the other things in my life.

I started thinking about this today as I was driving home. Thanksgiving is in two days, and we always make a lot of food because we like to eat.[120] We did most of the grocery shopping over the weekend, but there were a few last minutes items I still needed. I know that daring to step into a grocery store this close to a holiday is an act of both bravery and stupidity. I decided to attempt this act between classes. I figured that hitting the store around noon might provide me a window where it would be less packed since many people would still be at work. I had just over two hours. Even if the store was packed I should still have time to run everything home before my afternoon class. If I ran out of time, the weather is cool

---

[119] Keeping myself from responding to such remarks is my biggest act of self-restraint.

[120] Even though it's only the two of us, our menu includes, turkey, dressing, a sweet potation and potato mélange, greens, salad, green bean casserole, deviled eggs, cranberry sauce, cranberry "sauce" from a can, dinner rolls, and sweet potato pie. While we generally agree on most things, the cranberry sauce divide runs deep between us

enough that the groceries can sit in the car for a couple hours without worry about anything going bad.

Thankfully I timed my expedition just right and was able to get in and out of the store in under thirty minutes, meaning I had time not only to run the groceries home but also a few minutes to hang out with the Diva Dog. I live about a block from the river and often drive down the road next to it when I leave this particular store. I took that route today and found myself behind someone driving less than twenty five miles per hour. This road has a lot of curves so I'm used to people driving a bit more slowly or slowing down on the more intense curves. However, this person's driving took that caution to an extreme level. I found myself getting angry and telling them to hurry up. I had to consciously check that I wasn't driving too close to them in my desire to hurry home.

I eventually made it home and while unpacking the groceries started thinking about the experience. The river drive is beautiful, and today was a sunny day. There was still some snow on the ground, making for lots of glorious winter scenery. Why, then, did I feel the need to rush through the moment? Why didn't I take advantage of the beauty and the slow driving to practice being present? Because the other driver was driving so slowly and I am familiar with the twists and turns of the road, I could have practiced some deep breathing and enjoyed the moment of the drive instead of fuming at their inept driving.

While I should have taken my time, instead I fell into the busyness trap. Even though I had plenty of time to get home, unpack the groceries, and return to school, all I could focus on were all of the things I had to do – cleaning up the detritus of my daily life, organizing the holiday gifts I've already bought, making room in the refrigerator for all the foods we will be making, and all of those other things that seemed more important than the beauty of the moment.

Being present demands a constant shifting of our attention from those things we have been told should be important and instead toward those things that are important to us.[121] It requires us to remind ourselves to slow down. This is especially important when it comes to creativity. When I am painting and allow myself to get into a flow state, time becomes irrelevant. Even if I am painting quickly, it doesn't feel like I'm rushing. The physical act is separate from the spiritual experience of it. My hand may be jumping around the canvas and between dabs of paint, but my mind is present to the experience of the moment. When this happens, the act of creating becomes a meditative practice much like my more formal meditation practice.

Sometimes, however, I find myself rushing or thinking about rushing, just like my drive home today. In these moments, no matter how hard I try to reach a flow state, it never happens. Instead I find myself focused on getting done or finishing the painting or something else. In a sense, I guess when this happens I am letting busyness take over. The focus shifts to what I am doing and how quickly I can do it. I think of it as a chore or work, something that has to be done and not necessarily something that can or should be enjoyed. Instead of flowing into meditation, I am "busy, busy, busy." It's easy to ask, why would anyone choose this condition over the other? However, I don't think it's a conscious choice. I think it's part of the ways we've been conditioned to be in this world. This is another manifestation of that childhood lesson dictating that hard work is important and what determines our worth. We fall into the trap of believing that our value is connected to our financial status, not our emotional well-being.[122] Just imagine how different life would be if we valued emotional and mental health as much as we

---

[121] This is a lesson I need to learn in many ways. Not having fully learned it yet is why I have held onto the Professor title so long.

[122] Yet another reason why that Professor title hung around for so long.

do financial health, or to be even more daring, if we valued them more than finances.

The other sad thing about this is that if we are constantly busy and rushing through life are we really living life? Or does life just become another task on our never-ending list of things we must do and check off? We do and do and do without really being. Maybe that driver had it right after all, or at least maybe their slow driving was the reminder I needed for today. Take your time, slow down, and create. Allow yourself to be in this moment. In doing so, you may end up creating more than you could ever imagine. At the very least you might enjoy a few deep breaths and some glorious winter river views.

Just Say NO

What are things you can/should say NO to?

Maybe Nancy Reagan was onto something back in the 80s when she started telling everyone to just say no.

I am a strong proponent of establishing boundaries to protect yourself. It's important to know, understand, and respect your limits so that you can be the best you possible. I talk about this all the time to anyone who will listen or who just so happens to be in my general vicinity. I've given numerous presentations on the importance of saying no and establishing boundaries. I have a variety of workshops I've developed to help people learn how to establish boundaries and practice saying no to extraneous things in their lives. Of course knowing these things and putting them into practice in my own life aren't always the same thing.

Learning to say no wasn't a skill I was generally taught growing up as a child. There was the Nancy Reagan admonition to say no to drugs which also applied to other chemicals such as alcohol and nicotine. There was the say no to anyone attempting to take your virtue because a girl's virginity was a gift from God that should be cherished until you give it to your husband.[123] There was also the say no to random strangers who might approach you in public. All of

---

[123] I still cringe when I think about how often I heard the phrase "why would he buy the cow when he can get the milk for free?". How did no one really see the myriad levels of wrongness in projecting this message to young girls? I also cringe at the explicit heterosexist presumption in the sentiment, but both of these are stories best told in a different book or over strong adult beverages.

these messages revolved around safety, protecting yourself from the harm that chemicals or strangers could cause to your young body. Or with the case of girls' virtue, the numerous harms that would come to in this life and in the proverbial after life if you weren't a virgin on your wedding night.[124] Noticeably absent from these lessons, however, were any messages on saying no to protect your personal interests, mental health, and well-being.

Like many, if not most young girls, I was surrounded by messages on how to be a good little girl on my way to being a good little lady. My value as a girl depended in large part on my ability to follow and live up to these social mandates. I should look feminine by wearing dresses and skirts for at least some of the time. I should always be clean and tidy with a smile either on my face or at the ready. I should be soft in my outward demeanor by not raising my voice or being too knowledgeable in any one area. I should be accommodating and caring to those around me, especially those of the male persuasion. Most importantly for this meditation, I should not be selfish and always think of others first. As I matured, I internalized these lessons and still carry them with me today.[125] I also learned that the penalties for violating these expectations were meted out in many forms.

My best friends as a young girl were my neighbors Jimmy and Jeff. We would spend hours riding our bikes all over the city looking for our next adventure. In the summer we would play outside from right after breakfast until we were forced into bed in the evening. We became experts at getting ourselves into problems. I remember, for example, the first time my sister had a sleepover.[126] Jimmy, Jeff, and I spent the day rigging up the basement to scare her and her friends. We took apart some old speakers and rewired them so that when we

---

[124] I still don't understand this obsession with girls' virtue.

[125] I learned the lessons, but I never mastered them.

[126] I am forever sorry to my sister for the mess we made and to my mom who had to deal with all the angry parents.

triggered them they would make a creepy scratching sound. We hung strobe lights in the corners of the room with a remote switch we could turn on at the designated time.[127] We hung fishing line across the room and rigged up a fake bloody hand that would fly down the line so it looked like a disembodied hand was floating over them. Somehow we convinced their cousin Craig to put on a wolfman mask and wait outside the window of the room they would be sleeping in. The party kicked off and after a few hours, well after it was dark outside, we put our plan into action. We turned out the lights in the room, triggered the rewired speakers, turned on the strobe lights, tripped the bloody hand, and Craig put his face against the window and made howling sounds. Yes, it was a bit much, and yes, we all got in loads of trouble for it, but not once was my ability to do these things or keep up with the boys questioned.

Things began to switch, not surprisingly, once I got my first period – that moment when little girls instantly become women.[128] That year my grandfather passed away and part of the modest inheritance from his estate went toward purchasing a small above ground backyard pool. I loved being in the pool, and the three of us would spend hours playing in it. Then my first period arrived, and I learned that I wouldn't be able to join Jimmy and Jeff in the pool on period days. I remember sitting inside the back door on the basement steps looking out at them playing and crying because I was stuck inside. Around this same time, I also learned that our days of hanging out and causing trouble would be more limited now. As everyone loved to remind me, "It was time for me to stop being a tomboy and start being a lady."

I found myself increasingly surrounded by this same message from multiple sources. Activities that used to be considered normal and

---

[127] Thinking about all of these things now helps my first college major of Engineering make a bit more sense.

[128] Do you even have to ask if there is a rant that could accompany this?

part of my daily life were now taboo. My friends at school were no longer interested in playing tag football or Red Rover and instead spent all their free time trying to get the attention of the boys, even the boys that only a few months earlier we laughed at and made fun of. My friends also started telling me all of the ways I wasn't living up to my full potential and that I would never be happy if I didn't start acting properly. It became increasingly clear that in order to be a proper girl on her way to being a proper lady, live up to my potential, I would have to sublimate my interests and privilege those of boys on their ways to being men.[129] In other words, I learned not to say no except in those narrow parameters involving chemicals and chastity.

Putting my interests behind those of others isn't a lesson that only I learned and it's not one that is only learned by women even though that has been my focus in this reflection. I believe that sublimating your interests to those of others is a trait that crosses sex and gender categories. One of the common traits I see being held by people who have a hard time saying no is the desire to help others, either as part of their professional career or as part of their personal ethos. It seems there are always more people needing help than those willing to provide it.

As I have become more intentional in my mindfulness practices I have gotten better at saying no, some of the time. I have established strong boundaries in my professional life and no longer feel compelled to be checking my email all the time[130] or responding outside of standard work hours. I say no to projects that will consume too much of my time and for which I won't be compensated. I have stepped down from most of the boards I served

---

[129] This was also the time when I started questioning why I had to be with boys when all I really wanted was to be with girls.

[130] It's been a couple years now since I last checked email while walking down the stairs.

on and limit my service to a few select organizations where I know my input will have direct impact. The one area I have still not mastered saying no to, however, is to those individuals in need.

Today was a textbook example of how I still have work to do in this area. What I wanted to do today was spend the day thinking about all the food we would be eating for our Thanksgiving feast tomorrow while I flitted between painting and writing. Classes are out of session so I didn't have to be on campus. This could have been the perfect day to create and dream and be present to gratitude. Instead, however, I let my self-imposed guilt take over and scheduled several appointments and phone calls with pro-bono clients. I filled the day with things I had to do and which took time away from my creative desires. Instead of saying no I said yes many times over.

As I was driving into the office I kept up a running dialogue berating myself for doing this. I was angry, not at the clients who have very real needs and questions, but at myself. I fell, once again, into that trap of putting work before creativity.[131] I realized that this is another way I sublimate my interests. Even though I love having entire days where I can flit from creative project to creative project, I let that combination of working class and feminine guilt creep in and take over. I forgot to say no. If I'm being honest, I never even thought about saying no.

Being present to my creativity is important. It feeds my soul and by extension makes me a better person. In a very real sense, my creative pursuits are my daily air mask that provide me with the necessary life breath I need to be the best person I can be. Therefore, I need to remind myself of that message we all hear when we travel on planes – put your air mask on before helping anyone else. If my creative pursuits are my daily air mask, I need to put them first. I need to

---

[131] Will I ever internalize this lesson?

learn to say no. Actually, I need to learn to say no to saying no to my creative pursuits.

Meditation 23
Radical Gratitude

What does it mean to enact compassion for yourself and others
by living a life of gratitude?

Expressing gratitude to others is usually an easy task. Why, then, is it so hard to express gratitude to ourselves?

I think about gratitude often, both that which I feel and that which others share with me. When I first started my mindfulness practice, expressing gratitude regularly was one of the first practices I adopted. It makes sense to tell those we care for how much we appreciate them, even though we might not always do this. When I think about these expressions of gratitude, I think about more than telling them that we love them. Instead, I think about telling them why we are happy they are in our lives or how much having them in our lives is important to us.

I don't remember who I first expressed this form of gratitude to but I do remember their response. It is a response that I have now heard multiple times, "Oh no, what did you do or what do you want?" I'm not sure what response I expected or even if I expected any. I do know, however, this response was not something that had crossed my mind. I'm sure I stumbled through some response about how I just wanted to let them know how much I appreciated them.[132] I also laughed because knowing my history of rabble rousing it's not out

---

[132] Or at least I like to think my response was along these lines.

of the ordinary that I might have done something off or for which I would need help.

I've thought about this response to gratitude a lot since it first happened. I've never asked someone why that was their first response, but I kind of understand it. Receiving a compliment requires a vulnerability that is outside of our usual ways of being. We are used to hearing critical commentary in the form of "constructive" feedback. Even when the things being said are difficult, we know that ultimately they will help us improve and be better.[133] Over time we build up a protective veneer that helps shield us from the full negative feedback of such moments. In addition, it often feels like people are more willing to share negative comments rather than positive. As a teacher, I have learned to remind myself of this every time I read class evaluations. Students who are frustrated with me or the class are more likely to air those feelings in an anonymous form than in person.[134] This doesn't make reading such comments any easier, nor does it prevent me from veering into obsessing about why a particular student didn't like me.

What is less common, though, is receiving positive feedback of substance. By this I mean, the types of things that might be included in an expression of gratitude. It is one thing to be told how awesome your boots are[135], but it's something very different to be told how awesome you are. The first one, with its focus on your boots, is easy to distance yourself from by saying it's not about you but about an object, your boots. Even though you may have bought the boots, this illusion of distance is still feasible. Distance, real or illusionary,

---

[133] This doesn't include criticisms masquerading as constructive feedback. That's just mean.

[134] Not to mention that there's a growing body of evidence demonstrating that women and members of marginalized groups are evaluated more harshly that white men teachers.

[135] I have a slight obsession with boots so this might not be something others experience

isn't really feasible in the second one since the remark is clearly about you. Instead of being able to take the compliment for what it is, the compliment can create a sense of unease or a feeling that if we acknowledge the awesomeness of us we are being cocky or boastful.[136] Do I think such an acknowledgement is either of these things? Not at all. Do I find myself deflecting such remarks when they come my way? All of the time.

Another reason that a response such as, "Oh no, what did you do or what do you want?" occurs is connected to cynicism. In a consumer society where capitalism reigns and most things occur as transactions, everything feels or can feel like a transaction. This ideal is embodied in the axiom "you can't get something for nothing." When someone expresses gratitude for you by telling you how awesome you are, it feels like you are getting something for nothing. The cynical response to this, therefore, is to assume they want something in exchange. Too often, sadly, such compliments sometimes are indeed the first step in asking for a favor. The cynical response, then, is another form of protection. I think of it as a type of rhetorical sword – let me just jab first and get this request out of the way before I get hurt by thinking you were actually complimenting me.

In those early days of expressing gratitude, I was frustrated and sometimes hurt by these cynical responses. Intellectually, I understood why they occurred and that they weren't necessarily a reflection on me personally. Emotionally, however, they stung and took me back to all those moments as a young girl where my awkwardness made me the object of ridicule. I toyed with the idea of abandoning the practice in order to protect myself. Then I remembered there is that issue of not wanting to be a quitter and

---

[136] Even though not being boastful is a key tenet in those childhood lessons in being a lady, I don't think the feelings of unease is limited by sex or gender.

thinking I can make the world a better place and really believing that most people are genuinely good souls and all the other things that comprise me. Not quitting is also what I think of as the crux of radical gratitude.

I think of radical gratitude as more than the mere performance of gratitude. Performing gratitude is best embodied in the triteness of the phrase "attitude of gratitude." An attitude of gratitude is another one of those concepts that take an otherwise good practice and waters it down into something anyone can easily do. It becomes another task that can be easily completed by purchasing the right things that will help you achieve it. I think of it as a performance because the focus is all about demonstrating what a good person you are because you have the right attitude. Even though you may be expressing gratitude to someone else, it's really about you and the fact that you are doing this good thing. And you don't even have to express gratitude to be part of the performance of it, you can simply announce how good you are by wearing the message on your shirt.[137]

With radical gratitude, however, the focus shifts to the other person. This demands, then, that even in the face of cynical responses you keep pushing forward. Being present in these moments means that you can and should acknowledge that such responses feel prickly and upsetting, but it also allows you to acknowledge that the responses aren't about you. They are a manifestation of the other's insecurities and fears.

One of the interesting things about practicing radical gratitude is the way it shifts your way of being present in your life. I believe everything we do generates energy, so we have control over the types of energy we want to create. If we focus on the negative, the cynical,

---

[137] Yes, I might have a bit of an attitude about the whole marketplace of gratitude items.

then we are creating more negative energy around us and in our lives. Therefore, if we focus on the constructive positive messages of gratitude, we create more positive energy around us and in our lives. For example, I noticed that the more I told people thank you or how much I appreciate them, the more I found myself being the recipient of such messages. I also began to notice less of those cynical what do you want responses.

Even more important, though, is how I have seen practicing radical gratitude with others allows me to be more grateful to myself. This added benefit has been a trickle down bonus in my creative practices. In writing these meditations, I decided that for 30 days I was going to be present to my life in such a way that I noticed the lesson I was meant to learn for each day, whatever it was. In the late afternoon or early evening, then, I would write the meditation, letting the words flow through me as they came without trying to control them. My goal was to be a vehicle for the messages I receive. This isn't to say that the process has always been smooth. There have been days where I find myself picking up the phone to scroll through social media or other days where I feel that the words on the page most likely make no sense. However, I have also channeled some of that positive energy and expressed gratitude for being able to write, to think about things that are important to me, and to spend time with memories I haven't thought about in years.

An added bonus of being grateful to myself is that I find myself being even more creative. I am more open to try things that don't seem to make sense or that I'm not sure will work. I find myself wanting to attempt new techniques or use my tried and trusted tools in new ways. I'm not sure I fully understand the ways these things are connected to radical gratitude, other than my conviction that they are intimately connected. Perhaps, the only connection is myself?

By opening myself up to expressing and accepting gratitude, I embrace vulnerability. I allow myself to be vulnerable even when faced with the potential negativity of cynical responses. Each time I live through a moment of radical gratitude, I gain strength in knowing that I survived. I know that even though the recipient of my comment may not have been in a spot where they could hear the message for what it is, the energy of that message still resonates around them. They will carry it with them in their subconscious and be able to access it when they need it. The more I embrace vulnerability in moments like these expressions of gratitude, the easier it becomes to embody vulnerability in other moments of my life. This vulnerability helps me to brave stepping into new forms of expressing my creativity. It helps me overcome the fear of messing up or not being enough and allows me to dive into the unknown. It makes me a better and more fully rounded creative. And for that I am grateful.

Synchronicity

What does synchronicity look like in your life?

Allow yourself to be open to the meaningful moments and coincidences as they happen in your life.

Since I began intentionally practicing mindfulness I have added a variety of different ways to incorporate mindfulness into my life. Many of these practices are the usual suspects such as meditation, reflective journal writing, and acts of gratitude. There are some that I've created based on things specific to my life. For example, when I am starting a new painting I have a ritual I follow where I unwrap the canvas, thinking about the possibilities that await to be revealed on it. I love how blank canvases represent new beginnings and all the hope and promise encompassed within them. With each unwrapping I feel a rush of excitement. After I put the canvas on my easel, I anoint and bless it with a moon water and essential oil mix I keep in my studio. I spray this all over the canvas and chant, "bless this canvas with peace, love, and happiness." This ritual serves as a way for me to shift away from the demands of my work and regular life and move into the framework of intuitive painting. It provides a way for me to become present to the moment of creativity by becoming present to the blank canvas.

A couple years ago, I added an annual practice into my mindfulness life. Each year I choose a word for the year. I begin meditating on the new word of the year in the week between the Christmas holiday and the New Year holiday.[138] I open myself up to the energies that surge during this time and pay attention to any messages I receive. I simply let the process unfold as it will and usually within a few days into the New Year, the word meant to help guide my year will make itself known. I then memorialize the word through a creative process. For example, one year I felt called to create a mixed media painting that included the word and a symbol that appeared to me. Another year I created a sigil based on the word and a phrase that appeared. I don't overthink the creative product and instead focus on being present to my thoughts and emotions while creating.

This year, the word that appeared was synchronicity. I first noticed the word appearing during a Zoom meeting of creative women from around the world. We discussed lots of things, but for some reason that word kept jumping out at me. At one point we all decided to pull an oracle card for the others. The card I pulled was synchronicity. Over the next several days I kept seeing or hearing the word in the most random places – while standing in line at the grocery store, on a billboard next to the road, in the show I was binge watching at the time. When the word crept into my morning meditation several days in a row, I finally accepted that synchronicity was my word for the year. I did a reflective journal writing on synchronicity and why it would be important to me for the coming year.

At its most basic, I think of synchronicity as the process of finding meaning in the events and things happening around you. It's a blending of your internal and external worlds. Instead of dismissing coincidences as random events, synchronicity asks us to acknowledge the deeper meaning behind them. To be present to synchronicity, then, is to be open to seeing the meaningful coincidences when they happen. To me, living in synchronicity is

---

[138] That week where it's easy to get lost in the nothingness of between time.

simply another way living in mindfulness. You stay present to and aware of all the things around you.

The creative project that came to mind this year was a painting. During the ritual blessing of the canvas, I heard a message that I would return to this canvas throughout the year, finishing it as I began seeking the word for next year. In this way, the canvas acts as a portal receiving all of the synchronous moments and thoughts of this year. It contains all of that energy and as a portal, I will be able to access that energy every time I interact with it in the future.[139]

I first started thinking about synchronicity years ago when I read "The Celestine Prophecy." I took many lessons from it, but the one lesson that resonated the most deeply with me was the importance of being open to meaningful coincidences – synchronicity by another name. Even though this lesson moved me, like many other lessons it is one that I haven't always practiced or enacted. With all of the pressures and demands of living life and making a living, it is easy to fall into the trap of jumping from one task to the next, living your life as a series of check lists with boxes to be ticked off.[140] Being attuned to those random moments and exchanges that always occur is an easy thing to let fall by the wayside. It makes sense, therefore, that synchronicity forced itself into the forefront of my conscious thoughts.[141] For the last couple years I have been thinking and planning the next phase of my life. I've known for a while that I need to make changes in my professional life and have been thinking through what those might look like. I also know that opportunities often appear when we least expect them so being in synchronicity

---

[139] The painting is now complete and it is a veritable explosion of abstract colors and images.

[140] This feels like a full circle moment, taking me back to the early days of COVID lockdown with my daily check lists of tasks.

[141] It was persistent in its continual pushing until I recognized it.

allows you to be more open and receptive should the right thing cross your path.

The year isn't over yet, but the new year isn't that far away. Living in synchronicity for the past 11+ months has been a wonderful reminder of why I should walk in mindfulness and synchronicity all of the time. There have been little moments of synchronicity such as the time I said I wish I had some Trader Joe's creamy chocolate peppermint candies, and the next day a group of students dropped off a thank you present that included a box of them.

There have also been more significant moments of synchronicity. Someone asked me why I had stopped practicing law when I did. I explained that I had always hoped I could work to help victims of rape and domestic abuse find their way through the morass of the legal system and know that they had a strong advocate on their side. In passing, I said that if such a position would open up now, I could see myself jumping at it and going back into lawyer life. I didn't think much more about this conversation until a few months later when I was facilitating a continuing legal education seminar. After the program I was talking with a group of people over snacks and coffee. One of them mentioned how she was looking for someone to take over her role as a pro-bono victim's advocate for domestic abuse victims. I asked what the role entailed, and by the end of our conversation I indicated I might be interested. I then asked around to see what some of my trusted friends had heard about the role, and every single of them responded with, "are you thinking of doing that? You would be perfect for it."[142] Sometimes synchronicity hits you over the head, much like how it had to hit me over the head to make me realize it was my word of the year. A month later I was

---

[142] I sometimes wonder if I would ever get out of my own way without my circle of trusted friends who always push me to do the things I don't think I can.

interviewing for the position and am still serving as an advocate today.

I started thinking about synchronicity again today in another one of those random moments. Last night while watching tv, we saw a commercial for a fancy wet/dry floor cleaning system. I live in an old house with hardwood floors on the main level and carpeting on the second level. I hate housecleaning in general and really hate trying to keep up with the floors. It seems like I'm always dust mopping them even though they always seem to be dusty. This is especially frustrating in the mornings when the sun shines at just the right angle to highlight all of the monster size dust bunnies inhabiting the living room. After the commercial, I commented that perhaps I should think about getting one of those since it might simplify the process. We looked it up online and then went back to our random tv viewing.

This morning, however, the topic came up again. I mentioned that maybe I should check it out since I need to do something if I don't want to live with all those dust bunnies.[143] We were planning on doing errands later in the day and decided we would check it out while we were at Target. I forgot about it again, until we were in the store. We found ourselves by the vacuum aisle and decided to see if they had this particular model. They did, and it was on sale for $100 off the regular price. In that hitting me over the head way that my synchronicity works, there was only one left in stock, and the sale was only good through the end of the day. Instead of doing my usual overthinking and worrying about spending money on things I don't really need, I said let's do it and am now the proud owner of a fancy new wet/dry floor cleaning system.

---

[143] Thankfully Diva Dog is part poodle so she doesn't shed.

Today's shopping moment is a good reminder also of how if I let myself live my life without trying to control it, amazing things will happen. I don't have to worry about every little thing and should trust that I will find what I need when I need it. Not only should I breathe deep and create, but I should also breathe deep and live. Live into the moment and let the meaningful coincidences and synchronicities find their ways to me.

Meditation 25
Getting Lost

What areas in your life can you loosen up the plan
and let yourself momentarily get lost?

Wander, roam, take the random twists and turns that appear to you and remember the journey is sometimes more important than the destination.

Some of the best times in my life have occurred by accident when I have found myself lost without an exact, or any, clue of where to go next. In these moments I have wandered into areas I might never have seen otherwise and had conversations with people who I most likely would not have crossed paths with but for the fact of momentarily being lost. When I try to explain to others how I enjoy getting lost at times, I am usually met with a look of wonder and confusion. Some of the bolder, or you could say less kind, individuals will laugh at my observation and shake their head as if I'm making a joke. I used to try to explain myself, but now I simply shrug it off and feel bad that they will never get to know the joy of wandering someplace unknown.

There have been many times in my life where I have found myself with no clue where I am. One of my favorite memories of being lost is from when my daughter and I were in Italy with her youth orchestra. I was along on the trip not as an official chaperone but as an extra adult. Because I didn't have official chaperone duties, I didn't have to worry about following the (over)scheduled itinerary and could spend time roaming all over. Being in a foreign country with a language I didn't speak presented the perfect opportunity for lost expeditions. When we went to Padua, we decided to break away from the scheduled tour and walk around the town. We wandered into the Italian version of a farmer's market in one of the parks, and I bought a pair of platform wedge sandals that I wore for years until they finally fell apart.[144] The best part of the day, however, was when we saw a building with a beautiful stone archway in one wall. We went over to explore and found ourselves inside a courtyard in a tableau that was a highlight of our trip. There were lines of drying clothes strung across the expanse from one building to the next. Neighbor ladies hung out of windows talking with each other. In one corner a group of small tables and chairs were clustered where groups of men sat drinking and smoking and laughing. Small children ran back and forth in the area. All of this was accompanied by a young girl playing violin in the center of the courtyard. It was the type of scene that you would expect to see in a movie about old world Italy. And it was something that we would have never experienced but for our day of wandering around lost.

I appreciate that getting lost can be scary. During our Padua sojourn, for example, we wandered far away from the main downtown area. We knew we had to be on the bus at 6:00 p.m., and as the clock moved closer to that time we began to worry we might miss it. Thankfully, we crossed paths with a police officer and were able to communicate enough to get pointed in the right direction.[145] The fear we felt in that moment, is now part of the fond memory of the trip.

Another fear associated with getting lost is that engendered by the stranger danger messages that surround us, always reminding us to be on the alert. The gun and personal security system industries thrive on perpetuating the myth that life threatening danger is just

---

[144] I still dream about those sandals and wish I could have salvaged them.
[145] Six years of French lessons gave me enough of a basis in the romance languages to make up my own version of something that sounded Italian.

around the corner if you don't take steps to protect yourself. It is easy to fall prey to this culture of fear and assume that one misstep will result in the murder and mayhem that often dominates the news. From this perspective, getting lost is another thing to fear because if you don't know where you are how can you protect yourself?[146] I don't want to diminish the importance of safety, but the act of being lost is not immediately a pathway to not being safe.

Allowing yourself to take the occasional misstep and get lost can open up your eyes in interesting ways.[147] In addition to the possibility of seeing new places and meeting new people, you will learn more about yourself. Being lost forces you to navigate your way home. It requires you to be calm when fear would seem to be the easier answer. It demands that you be present in the world differently than your normal way of being, which in turn prompts your synapses to spring to life in different ways. It allows you to see yourself and the world differently. Channeling this energy into your life is a form of mindful presence that can be harnessed in many ways.

When I was learning to drive one of the lessons my dad made me practice repeatedly was the ability to find my way home from anywhere. As a child of the 1970s, this meant looking at a paper map to figure out where I was before determining a route home. I didn't always appreciate the significance of these lessons in the moment. Like most teenagers I would have preferred hanging out with my friends or even going to my part-time job at McDonald's rather than spending my Saturday driving random places and then trying to get home. In retrospect, though, these moments are some of my favorite memories of my dad. Since it was only the two of us, we would pass

---

[146] This message is exacerbated by classist and racist narratives connected to place and the "neighborhoods you should avoid."

[147] Even though I'm focusing on literally getting lost, as I'm navigating my exit from the academy I find myself metaphorically lost at times as well. I know where I've been and that I don't want to go back there. However, I'm still not sure where I'm going.

the time talking about whatever arbitrary thing happened to come to mind. I loved to read, and my dad was working his way through many of the classic books after having earned his GED later in life, so many of our conversations were about books we were reading or hoped to read. We made jokes about the weird and often surprising detritus we saw scattered along the sides of the road. We critiqued the driving skills we saw being demonstrated by the drivers that sped past us.

Getting lost became more than just a way for me to learn how to navigate and get home, it was also a way for us to pause our individual lives and be present to and with each other.

I know these moments were the reason why I love maps, old school maps printed on paper. It was only after reflecting on getting lost that I realized how those early days of driving likely planted the seeds that grew into my love of getting lost. Today, one of my favorite parts of each journey is sitting down with real maps and charting out the best and alternate ways to get to where I'm going.[148] With the ease of access to GPS navigation now, this process isn't really necessary but I still love it. Getting lost today, with our easy access not only to GPS navigation but any other information we want to access, is more difficult but not impossible.

I'm thinking about getting lost and how important it is because even with using GPS navigation I found myself lost today. We have been talking about going to this witchy crystal store that we found on Facebook for a couple months now. It's located just under an hour away so we thought it would make a fun little day trip. Each time we planned the trip, though, something happened that made us cancel. The fates, or maybe synchronicity, aligned today, though, and we headed out. I had already looked over the various routes available

---

[148] I maintain a AAA membership mostly so that I can order Trip Ticks and the routes they chart for me.

and decided on the one I wanted to take. The quickest and most direct route was the highway, but I hate highways for their sameness and lack of interesting sights, despite their convenience. Whenever possible, I choose backroads and more scenic options even though they add time to the trip. However, I firmly believe the journey is as important as the destination, and we should honor the journey whenever we can.

We headed out of the house and after a quick stop for gas and caffeine headed down the chosen route. The first steps were familiar territory that we drive fairly often so we enjoyed looking for any new buildings or other things along the road. After our first big turn, the navigational directions told us to go straight where I had expected we would be turning again. Instead of stopping to look over everything I decided we should go wherever it took us. We ended up driving through lots of little areas I had never seen before. We didn't have much traffic to contend with so we didn't have the pressure or stress of other drivers. For most of the journey we were lost. We knew we were moving in the generally correct direction; however, if we were forced to explain where we were at any given moment, it would be impossible. I felt invigorated in our lostness and commented how much fun this was turning out to be. To make our moment of being lost complete, we ended up initially driving right past the witchy crystal store and had to turn around and head back to find it.

Getting lost today reminded me how important it is to sometimes let yourself go and allow yourself to roam and wander. When it comes to creating, it can be easy to fall into the trap of thinking everything needs to be mapped out, to think you have to know the destination and each exact step along the way before you begin. I spent years approaching my writing this way. I would dedicate time to gathering all of my research and make detailed notes of which material I was likely to use where. I would then prepare step by step outlines of each part of my argument. This process served me well and helped me write many things. However, I realize now how the process also constrained me by making me feel locked into the map. When inspiration would strike, it would have to be added to the map. As I have embraced living into my creativity I have found that letting go of the map is easier. When I allow myself to get lost, either on the page or on the canvas, I find that even though the destination may differ it is often better, just like the Padua courtyard.

Make Mistakes

How do you feel about making mistakes?

Make all the mistakes and breathe into the possibilities and opportunities they create.

Mistakes in life happen. They are part of our sameness as human beings. When we make a mistake it can be easy to fall prey to that internal critical voice and beat ourselves up or think we are a failure and all those other things that arise from such negative self-talk. I wonder, however, what would happen if we changed our perspective on mistakes. Instead of assuming they are automatically wrong and a negative occurrence, how would our understanding of them change if we considered mistakes as opportunities?

It's important to clarify what I mean by mistakes in here. There are some errors, mistakes, that are potentially life threatening such as serving peanuts to an individual allergic to them or stepping on the gas pedal when you mean to step on the brakes. In both of these situations, the possible consequences of such actions can be devastating. Not only will another person likely be harmed, but the residue of being the cause of such harm is likely to stick with you and cause serious long-term emotional damage. These types of mistakes are not the things I'm thinking about with this meditation. Instead, I'm thinking about those little hiccups that occur in life and don't cause serious or permanent damage.

I think about my own connection to mistakes quite often. I am highly competitive with myself and hold myself to high standards.

While I don't believe in or seek perfection, I do expect certain standards from myself. At times, these exacting standards can immobilize me such as with the abandoned manuscript on my dining room table or the canvases stacked against the walls of my living room. I keep these things out in the open to remind myself that mistakes happen. At other times, the mistake sets off my inner critic with a series of self-chastising commentary.[149] If I don't shut the voice down immediately, I can easily fall prey to her harsh words and begin to believe the lies they spread. In my mindfulness practice journey, I have intentionally committed myself to working on being present when these moments happen so that I can work on shifting my focus.

One of the mantras I have for myself is no mistakes, only opportunities. I say this to myself regularly as a reminder not to fall prey to the negativity of the inner critic.[150] When I started my journey to embrace my creativity, this mantra became even more important to me. I also realized that my mantra was probably influenced by Bob Ross. My great grandmother lived with us for a few years during my childhood. In her younger years she was a master at ceramics and porcelain. I remember wandering around her basement for hours being fascinated by the tools of her trade. At the bottom of the stairs was the kiln she used to fire her creations. As you moved into the room, you would enter her giant workspace – a big square table covered with paints and brushes and works in progress. Along the walls were shelves filled with molds for the porcelain creations she would make. She passed away while I was still fairly young, and I often think about how much I could have learned from her if I had only been born a few years earlier. I still have several of her porcelain and ceramic creations throughout my house.

---

[149] Peggy can be quite loquacious at times.
[150] Like everything else in my life, this is a work in progress. Some days, no matter how many mantras I cite, the negativity wins.

When upkeep of the house became too much for her, she was forced to sell it and all of her supplies. I don't know where they ended up, but I hope they found a happy home where they continued to find years of creative happiness. When she lived with us, she continued to express her creativity with crocheting and embroidery, but I think she missed her days of painting and creating porcelain pieces. She is the one who introduced me to the glorious weirdness of Bob Ross. We would watch together when I would spend time with her in her room. She would comment on his processes and things she might do differently. His version of no mistakes was what he called "happy little accidents." A happy accident occurs when your brush slips or you make a mark you don't like. Instead of viewing it as a mistake, he would assert it was a happy little accident and demonstrate how you could turn the mark into a bird or a happy flower.

When I paint, I am generally pretty good at adopting the Bob Ross approach and let my mistakes become part of the final product. For example, I have a Green Tara painting hanging in my bedroom who was made better by such a mistake. Surrounding her head is a circle reminiscent of a head piece. It went through various manifestations before I realized it wanted to be a circle of flames representing her energy and strength. I dipped my brush in the paint on my palette, and as soon as I made the first stroke on the canvas realized my mistake. Instead of dipping into the crimson, I had dipped into the medium magenta next to it. Whereas crimson is a deep rich red, medium magenta is a darker pink. Though related, they are clearly two different colors. I breathed deeply and stepped back to look at the overall effect. While it was different than originally intended, it wasn't bad. I used up the rest of the magenta on my brush[151] and then went back in and added in some of the originally intended

---

[151] You never want to waste paint as it's a valuable resource.

crimson. The end result exuded a depth and richness I would have missed but for my mistake.

I started thinking about all of these things today while cooking, another form of meditation and creative expression I wish I had more time to practice. Even if I am working from a recipe, I don't worry about exact procedures or measurements and instead let my intuition guide me. The acts of gathering ingredients, chopping, and combining them are as deeply contemplative as when I sit to meditate.

I love homemade soup and use any excuse to make a big pot of it. Even though I live alone during the week, whenever I make soup I make enough to feed a family of four with plenty of leftovers. I believe you can never have too much soup, as demonstrated by the myriad individual servings sitting in my freezer at any given moment. Today's soup making endeavor revolved around the leftover turkey carcass from Thanksgiving. I began the process last night by putting the carcass in the crockpot with celery, onions, carrots, and a beautiful bouquet garni of the leftover fresh herbs from our holiday cooking, accompanied by a handful of black peppercorns. I let it slow cook overnight and woke up to a house filled with the smells of turkey stock.[152]

I decided today's soup was going to be a turkey and dumpling one based on a recipe for chicken dumpling soup I stumbled upon a few years ago. The trick is using gnocchi instead of making your own dumplings. You still get the starchy goodness that you would with a dumpling but without the extra work of making your own dumplings. I sauteed my vegetables in butter and added in all of my

---

[152] If you haven't tried the crockpot for stock, you must do so. The slow cooking creates a depth of flavor that is hard to match unless you have an entire day to be at the stove.

spices, including more pepper. After letting it simmer for a few minutes, I added flour to the mixture. This is another trick I have adopted to help thicken the soup without needing to make a roux. After a few more minutes I added in my glorious stock and a bit of cream. While stirring this mixture and dreaming of the amazing dinner I was going to have this evening, something grabbed my attention. I realized the smell was different than it had been in the past. I kept stirring while reviewing the steps I had taken. This is when I realized my mistake. The recipe calls for thyme, and in my soup craving induced haze I had added tarragon instead of thyme. The smell that had pulled me from my soup meditation was the distinct licorice smell of tarragon.

Before my inner critic took over, I rummaged through my collection of spices to confirm. When I cook I like to place the containers of spices I've used in a basket on the counter next to me. This way, they are easily accessible should I need to add more. I thought that maybe in the distraction of my soup fantasies, my sense memory had taken over and I had actually used thyme as directed. A quick review of the basket contents confirmed that my nose was right, and I had grabbed tarragon instead of thyme. I closed my eyes and took a few deep cleansing breaths trying to stave off Peggy's comments. I like tarragon and used to incorporate it into many of my recipes, so it's not like this mistake would result in something horrible, or at least that's what I hoped. I kept stirring and thinking about what I should do. After a few more deep breaths, I remembered my no mistakes, only opportunities mantra. Maybe the act of grabbing the tarragon was my inner intuitive creative side pushing me to try something new. Even though I had made this recipe several times, that doesn't mean I have to keep making it the same way.

I am happy to report that after several more minutes of cooking and letting the ingredients' flavors emerge, my taste test of the soup made me smile. The mistake was a textbook happy accident that means I now have another option for how to make this soup in the future. I am writing this before dinner and can smell the soup simmering on the stove. The lingering tarragon essence in the air is making me excited to enjoy this new version of my old favorite.

Embrace the Grey and Live Into the Ambiguity

In what areas of your life are you taking the easy answer as a way to try to control your future?

The world isn't black and white, no matter how much we may try to make it so. Everything is complex and nuanced, so we need to learn to love the many shades of grey that comprise being human.

Another one of my go to mantras is "embrace the grey and live into the ambiguity." I have been saying this to myself for years. I was reminded of it today when I found myself repeatedly saying, "I can't give you a yes or no answer because the situation is a lot more complicated than that. There are many possibilities." Each time I was met with a sigh of frustration.[153] I understand the desire to want concrete, yes or no answers. If I know exactly what I am supposed to do or how to do it, then it's easy to believe that everything will work out for the best. Except, of course, humans are complicated, and life is messy. Things often don't work out the way we anticipate even when think we have the right answer.

Being in the unknown, the ambiguous, is scary. To move forward or do something without knowing exactly what the outcome will be can be terrifying. Embracing the grey can cause immobilizing fear. However, do we ever really know what the future will bring? Is knowing what is always going to happen the way that we really want

---

[153] And each time I had to remind myself not to sigh back in my own frustration.

to live? In a culture where we are surrounded with messages telling us about all the scary people out there and all the scary things that can happen to us, not knowing exactly what will happen can seem like an impossible moment to navigate. It seems easier, therefore, to counter our immobilizing fear by seeking a black and white answer. However, an easy answer isn't necessarily a good answer. I would argue that the easier an answer is, the less likely it is to be a good answer.[154]

For the past few years, I've ignored my own advice of accepting the complexity of life and living into the grey. Despite being increasingly unhappy with my professional life, I stuck with the easy answer by sticking with my tenured professor position. I had myriad reasons to leave – low pay, around the clock calls on my time, the demands of grading coupled with the emotional labor of helping students understand not all work earns an "A," and my general dissatisfaction with the increasingly consumerist approach to education. I love teaching, so it was easy to fool myself into thinking that merely having the opportunity to teach was enough for me to thrive. I could ignore the many negative signs and instead focus on the reasons I've stayed this long – steady paycheck, benefits, long breaks between semesters.[155] Staying is easy.[156] Leaving means not only embracing the grey and living into ambiguity but also giving up control, even if that control is illusory.

The more I fight living into the ambiguity of my life, the less control I have. I can tell myself that I am choosing to stay so I can be in charge. I can also tell myself that I am in control. However, this type

---

[154] When I first wrote this, I wrote "good" as "god." I didn't catch this mistake until editing. I feel like there's a whole other meditation wrapped up in that missing "o."
[155] Although this is really only an illusion of a benefit as the emails keep coming and the pressure to research and publish never ceases.
[156] In my head I'm singing Hamilton lyrics where Washington reminds Hamilton that dying is easy and living is hard.

of control is control in name only. It's another manifestation of that mythical control of life and the future. If I know what is happening then I am in charge, and if I'm in charge then I'm in control. In order to make this illusory control happen, I have to ignore all those reasons to leave and stick with the easy answer of my job. I have to fool myself into believing that knowing I have a steady paycheck and health insurance, I can control my future. Except of course that life doesn't operate like this. No matter how much I may know about something and no matter how tightly I cling to that paycheck, I still have no control over the future. I can't predict the future as much as I might want to. Living into the ambiguity means living in the unknowing, a state of suspension.

What's especially interesting is that I know that being present to the ambiguous in creativity is essential to the process. A perfect example is this particular meditation in its first draft. When I started writing these meditations I had no plan or idea what they were going to be. My intention in the beginning was simply to sit down each day and write around 1700 words on whatever topic came to me, allowing whatever messages the universe had for me and to channel them into my writing. After a few days, I found myself falling into a pattern of writing about the interconnections of self, presence, and creativity. I realized that the process was a meditative one and the stuff I was writing were meditations. I didn't change my writing process, though, and have continued to sit down daily and open myself to whatever message occurs.

Today, however, I came into the process differently. After having the same conversation over and over with multiple students and clients, I decided I must write about my mantra of "embrace the grey and live into the ambiguity." I have been saying this to myself and others for years and decided it was time to share it with others. In other words I was trying to control the situation and therefore the outcome by having a solid black and white approach. This made the writing process much more frustrating and the resulting draft from that process was an embarrassment of writing. I know that not all drafts are going to be smoothly written and that some drafts will need to be completely rewritten to be presentable. I also know that whenever I try to write within a box or a constraint that the final result is less than ideal. Some days, however, I forget all of this and try to control the outcome – even when I'm writing about living into the ambiguity

I keep thinking back to those early days of painting Buddha when I struggled with not knowing what to do. Part of those struggles were me learning the technical basics of painting with acrylics. In my naïve eagerness, I believed that putting lots of paint on my brush would make it easier to work. I now know that all that extra paint was a significant part of the problems I was having in achieving the effect I wanted. Despite this struggle and my days of working on getting Buddha's nose shaded the way I wanted, I found a way to keep living into the ambiguity of the moment. I didn't try to control the moment and instead embraced the greyness of it. The more I have reflected on this moment today, the more I realize that it was easier for me to live into the ambiguity of painting Buddha because I wasn't an expert. I was still learning and perfecting my technique so not knowing the answers was to be expected. With my profession and my writing, I'm already considered an expert[157] so I should know about way around the ambiguous things and be able to find answers. Even though I know I'm human and that mistakes are an inherent part of the human condition and that perfection is an illusion, I fell into the trap of seeking the easy answer.

As I'm writing this, I've been thinking about why did this happen today? Why, despite my mantra, did I fall into this old pattern? And in asking those questions I find myself wanting answers. I want to

---

[157] Or at least experienced enough to know some answers.

know. I want the black and white. I want the answer for how to prevent this from happening next time, because there will be a next time. I will have another stressful day where I have to repeat the same thing over and over. I will have another creative project that I feel I must control from the beginning if I am going to complete it. I will forget my own mantra and slip out of being present in the moment and instead obsess about the future.

I wish I had the answer for how to prevent this from happening, but then again if I did have that answer I wouldn't need to be writing this meditation.[158] Maybe part of the answer is accepting that I don't have the answer, and in fact, I don't have a lot of answers. Even though I am writing these meditations for myself and for others, I don't have to have all the answers. I can not only live into the ambiguity but I can also accept that I am a human with the inherent limitations and failings that are part of the human condition. I can forgive myself and try again tomorrow. I can, and I must, embrace the grey and live into the ambiguity.

---

[158] I wonder if there even is an answer to such a situation. There's the easy answer of remember your mantra, but I had that mantra today as well.

Not Knowing

How do you find the courage to move forward
when you don't know how?

Not knowing. Sometimes it's ok not to know, and in those moments you have to find the courage to move forward.

I don't know what to write about today. It's only Tuesday afternoon, but it already feels like I've lived an entire week. Classes are in the final days before the end of the semester so the grading is piling up, and I am expending a lot of emotional labor helping students worry less. My legal advocacy work is ramping up as the stress of the holidays plays out in the ways people interact with each other. I've also been having odd dreams that take me to intense environments where I have to fight to survive. I don't really know who my foes are in these dreams, only that they cause me a lot of fear. These dreams are so interactive that I find myself waking up to exercise credits already recorded on my Apple watch.[159] All of this extra work and stress is causing my mind to feel like it's on constant overdrive.

Life happens and the busyness of life ebbs and flows. I know that each time a flow like the current one occurs it will soon be followed by an ebbing where time seems to expand. Even with this current flow moment, I know that the ebb is just around the corner and will happen at the latest in a week and a half. Living through these flow moments, is still challenging, however. It is easy to jettison to the

---

[159] If I could find a way to intentionally make this happen it could be the start of the next exercise trend and the perfect get rich quick scheme.

side my mindfulness practices. When I already feel like I don't have enough time to return all the emails and voicemails that are piling up, spending thirty minutes doing nothing seems wasteful even though I know that meditating is not an act of doing nothing. It is tempting, however, to steal that time away and devote it to something "more important" such as decreasing the volume of messages in my inbox.[160] Likewise, it is easy to fall into my old habit of leaving my creative practices to be done after my work. Splashing paint onto the page seems like an unnecessary frivolity when there are so many other, more important things that need doing.[161]

As I'm writing all of this, I can't help but reflect on how living through this flow moment is another reminder of the enduring strength of those early messages about the value and work and worth. What counts as work are those tangible tasks connected to your job first and your home/family second. Only after they are complete should tasks connected to myself be considered. Even though I know this is utter crap, in moments of flow and stress like the current one, it is easy to forget that caring for my self, physically and emotionally, is at least as important as caring for my professional obligations.[162] If I'm being honest, attending to the self is even more important than attending to work. If I don't take care of myself, eventually my mind or body or both will say enough and force me to take care of myself, meaning that those professional obligations will still need to wait.

---

[160] I long for those early, naïve days of email when we believed the hype that we would have less work with it.

[161] In the spirit of transparency, I'm leaving that thought in here. I know that creating is necessary, but for a bit this thought took up a lot of mental space.

[162] This is another reminder why this is my time to leave academia. While there are many messages filled with talk of appreciating the need for work/life balance, there is also the reality of the demand of ongoing accessibility coupled with way too many emails.

Knowing all of this and acting on it are two different things. My success has occurred in part by being able to complete the tasks presented to me. I was the good student who always turned in her work on time. When I first practiced law I was the associate attorney who was always first in and last out of the office. As a tenure track professor, I banished the word "no" from my vocabulary and took on every committee or other task asked of me. I showed up in all the right places at all the right times and spoke to all the right people. Once a week I would walk through every building on campus, greeting everyone I saw so that I could visibly demonstrate my dedication to the life of a professor. I remember that when I was putting together my tenure dossier and discussing it with a colleague from another department she commented that she thought I already had tenure because it seemed like I had been there so long with all the things I was involved in. While all this work worked for me, it also took a physical toll on me. Every semester by the time I was finishing up final grades, I would find myself sick with a bug that would force me to bed for days. My body called bullshit on my refusing to rest and forced the issue.

Likewise, in busy moments like now devoting time to creativity seems wasteful and impossible. Creative time isn't work time and therefore needs to stay in its lane and wait its turn. I know that's not true, but I still struggle with believing it. Even more difficult to navigate, however, is the impossible part of creating. Other than basic house cleaning tasks, my work primarily consists of mental labor. I am either figuring out ways to distill complex information and present it to diverse audiences or figuring out possible solutions to difficult and dire situations that seem to be impossible. I spend a lot of time reading and processing information. I get headaches just like most people, but I also have times where my brain just hurts. Unlike a headache which has a physical cause, a brain hurt comes from over use. I think of brain hurts as akin to the muscle aches that occur when you work out extra hard or use your muscles in a different way. When my brain hurts, the last thing I want to do is engage in an activity that requires me to use it even more, even if it is an activity I love.

One of the results of brain hurt moments is what happened when I sat down to write this meditation. My brain says, "enough, I'm not giving you anything." In other words, I don't know what to write or paint or draw or otherwise create. Intellectually I understand why this happens, but I also know that moments of stress like this are the ones where I most need to create. If I can find a way to push past the resistance of thinking I don't have time or shouldn't devote time to create, I will find that I have created more time for myself. If I can push past the not knowing what to write or paint or draw or otherwise create, the end result will surprise me.

Intimately connected to the resistance of creating in moments of not knowing is that focus on product not process. Not knowing what to create simply means you don't have a plan. You don't have an end goal. It doesn't mean you can't create, it simply means you don't know what you're creating. The interesting thing about this is that my whole approach to creating intuitively is grounded in not having to know. The aim is to be present to the process of creating and trusting that the process will reveal the end goal. I have loads of experience that this works and that when I allow the process to unfold, I am always pleased with where it takes me. However, knowing this and believing it are two different things, and ultimately that seems to be part of the lesson that I am meant to take from this meditation – have faith in myself and in the process.

The question then of how do you find the courage to move forward when you don't know how seems especially poignant today. How do I find the courage to push aside those lifelong messages that tell me that focusing on myself needs to be a secondary goal? This is another one of those things that I wish I had the answer to because then I would shout it to the masses. What I can do is tell you my process for completing this meditation. While I was walking back to my office from class, I tried to motivate myself to write this meditation before my next class. This two hour space in time is the best option to be able to focus today, so I needed to use it wisely. I immediately pushed back at myself and said I don't know what to write about. As soon as I said it I decided to start from there and see what happened. The other thing I did was promise myself I only had to sit and write for 15 minutes. If after that time I still didn't know what I was doing or was still feeling frustrated I gave myself permission to stop and return to it later. I use promises like this as a way to push myself out of the funk of the moment while also being gentle with myself.[163] It forces me forward and usually ends up with me creating for far longer than the minimum time I set. And as this meditation demonstrates, I went from not knowing what to write to writing an entire meditation.

The key to creating in moments like this is finding the strength and courage to push past the moment of not knowing. Another key is reminding yourself that there will always be more work and even if you find a way to get through all those e-mails and voicemails there will always be more tomorrow. Let's be realistic, there will likely be more within moments of responding to the last one. Even more important, however, is reminding yourself that you are important and you are worthy of even more care and attention than those tasks. Your creative energy is important. Let it out and let it fly free. The energy you exert through creating will come back to you multifold and help you muddle through the onerous tasks. It's ok not to know, sometimes not knowing takes you to wonderful places.

---

[163] The only way I can work out on many days is with a promise of it will only have to be 15 minutes.

Meditation 29
Say Yes

What can you say yes to today?

Sometimes we need to be reminded to say yes and that saying yes is a good thing.

I hear and see lots of messages about the importance of establishing boundaries and saying no. As a woman who was socialized in a culture that demands that women be feminine which means acting as caregivers at all times and that we put other's interests before our own, I appreciate these reminders. I think it's important that we be reminded that saying no is not only acceptable but also sometimes necessary. Even though I firmly believe in boundary setting and no saying, I still have moments where I struggle and feel that if I say no I am being mean or will be thought of as a lesser person. [164] Intellectually I know that these thoughts are self-imposed and not grounded in reality, but they still feel real, very real. Despite all this attention to saying no, we don't see as much attention to saying yes.

It might seem counterintuitive to think that we have to be reminded to say yes, and perhaps it is. However, there are moments in our lives when saying yes is the last thing we want to do. I started thinking about this today as I was planning out my day and trying to figure out how I was going to fit in all of the things that need to be done, knowing there simply isn't enough time. In the afternoon I had a

---

[164] There are many times and places when you must say no – abuse, violence, toxic environments. My thoughts in here are not meant to disavow situations like these. There are times when your first impulse to say no needs to be acknowledged.

meeting scheduled with a long-time friend. The plan was to catch up and eat some food. Before COVID we would try to do this every few weeks, but for the last few years we have not been able to return to our routine. We have both talked about how much we missed those times of friendship and sharing. We finally decided to dive back in and meet for food and friendship. When we scheduled this meeting time a few weeks ago, I had no clue how busy I would be when it finally came around. All morning I was tempted to text that we need to reschedule. I resisted the urge to send that text and decided instead that even though I know he would understand the need to reschedule, I would say yes.

In stressful and busy times like this moment it seems like the easiest answer is to say no.[165] It is tempting to once again privilege work over everything else, including myself. I find that saying no is an especially tempting prospect now that it is becoming more socially and culturally acceptable to do so. Not saying no in this situation kinda feels wrong, especially when I am surrounded by messages reminding me that empowered women say no. When I think about it like this, I find myself pausing, being sad, getting mad, and breathing deeply. Once again that mindset that work must come first creeps its way into my existence, and with it comes the accompanying guilt and self-flagellation that seem to be part of its posse, like they are a messed up version of the Three Musketeers. Being able to overcome these messages and years of indoctrination requires an intentional action.

One of the founding principles of improv theatre is the concept of saying "yes and." In improv you and your partner[166] create the "play." What is being performed is spontaneous and developed through the back and forth interactions of the players. Each person

---

[165] Another reminder that easy answers aren't good answers.
[166] Improv is not limited to only two players at a time, but to simplify our discussion here I'm only going to work with two

works off the cues given to them from their partner. For example, your partner may say, "I was shocked when I first realized you were an alien." Your responsibility is to then respond to the cue, adding more information, and then giving the next cue to your partner. The back and forth process continues until the performance is brought to an end. The concept of "yes and" is imperative to keep the flow going and to help develop the richness and depth that make for good performances. Even when you don't like the cue or aren't sure what to do with it, you say "yes and" before adding more information. In this example, you might not want to be an alien and may have been thinking the performance would go in a different direction. However, you would fight the urge to reject the cue. Instead of saying no you might say, "Yes, and I sometimes forget that I am an alien since I have been around humans for so many years now. I still don't understand how you figured out I was an alien. You must have x-ray vision." The concept of "yes and" allows for a spontaneity that is fun and interesting. It is also a good concept to add to our everyday life.

Unlike the improv example, we are most likely not going to have people putting us in the position of acting like aliens.[167] We are likely, however, to be confronted with moments and situations where our initial impulse is to say no, like my moment today. The easy answer to finding more time in my schedule today would have been to say no to meeting my friend. This makes perfect sense with all the demands on my time, but, once again, the easy answer is rarely the best answer. Instead, I said "yes and." Specifically I said, "Yes I am busy and stressed and need a few more hours in the day today, and I need to eat and refresh myself and interacting with friends helps me maintain my mental health." Saying "yes and" forced me to consider the situation from a more expansive perspective and helped

---

[167] However, wouldn't such an activity be a fun way to spend a day? In a similar vein, it would be interesting to learn that we actually have aliens walking amongst us. I'm pretty sure there is an active conspiracy theory currently advocating this.

me realize that keeping our meeting would be the best thing in the long run, and it was. Not only did we have a wonderful time catching up, but we also got to enjoy pizza, one of my all-time favorite foods. Even better, I talked through some of the ideas for creative projects I've had rolling around in my head, which helped me prioritize which ones to start on now and which to delay until a better time.

Saying yes also allows us to be more fully present in our lives. Busy times are going to happen. We are sometimes going to be forced to do things we would rather avoid. There will be moments where we want to push back, run away, or simply say nope to what is happening in our life. Life, however, is messy and complicated. It isn't always going to be puppies and rainbows and unicorns and all the things we enjoy and love.[168] When we learn to say yes to those messy and complicated parts of life, we will more fully appreciate those times when life is lived as if wearing rose colored glasses.

Just as saying "yes and" in improv creates a richer and deeper performance, saying yes in life creates a more rich and textured life. We may find, like my meeting today that the thing we were convinced we should say no to was the exact thing we needed in this moment. I think this meditation showed up today to remind me that I need to attend to my departure from the academy. Every time I've reflected on it or started to take steps toward making it happen, I've stopped myself. The reasons to say no to leaving are important things to acknowledge; however, they are not necessarily reasons significant enough for me to stay. Instead, I can and should say "yes and" to them. "Yes, health insurance is important, and you will figure out how to buy it on your own." "Yes, you have bills to pay, and you have other ways to earn money." Ultimately, saying yes allows us to

---

[168] Although I wouldn't say no to living in such a world.

be present to the troubles or stress or other things we are avoiding but also forces us to accept them.

Saying yes isn't limited to improv and life. It should also be a pivotal part of our creative journey as well. I find that in every creative endeavor I tackle I have moments of extreme resistance. For example, in writing this meditation I have had several times where I have toyed with the idea of scrapping the whole thing and starting over. I have been convinced that what I thought was going to be a good meditation is actually just a bunch of random words that I'm stringing together.[169] In all honesty, I'm pretty sure if this meditation wasn't focused on saying yes that I would have already ditched it and started over. The saying yes, however, has helped me create something that I didn't even know I needed. It has helped me see that despite all the deep diving inner work I've done I still have pockets of resistance that can creep up and cause me to work against myself.

---

[169] And yes, I see the inherent irony in those thoughts as I'm writing about saying yes to the things you think you should avoid.

Meditation 30
Endings and Beginnings

What things do you need to end in your life to make
space for beginning something new?

Every ending isn't the final moment. Often the ending is less of a door closing and more of a window opening onto something new.

When I started writing what has now become these meditations, I thought I only wanted to accept the challenge of writing 50,000 words in thirty days. I realized within a few days, though, that these writings were the next step in my journey of embracing my creativity and leaving the academy. For 30 days, I forced myself to come back to the page and honestly grapple with all of the random thoughts that had been taking up space in my mind for the last few years. That entire time, I knew that this day, the final day would arrive. After all, it's a 30 day challenge so by definition at the end of those 30 days you have either completed the challenge or not. Yet when I confronted the reality of this being the last meditation, I found myself feeling sad and a tad lost.

Sitting down every day to write quickly became a ritual,[170] a ritual I grew to love. Most days I would write in either the late afternoon or early evening. I would sit in my favorite reading chair with my computer resting on a pillow on my lap and Diva Dog snuggled in by my side. Each day I would wonder if today was the day my words

---

[170] I love a good ritual as much as I love a good personal challenge.

would fail me.[171] Yet even though there were some days where the words didn't flow as smoothly as usual, somehow they still always came. I found myself looking forward to being present to this daily moment of creativity and reflection. I was excited to see what memories would arise and where they would take me.[172] Today, however, I kept putting off the writing. I had a break while on campus where I could have written, but instead I decided to grade.[173] When I came home, I had another opportunity to write but I created many things that "had" to be done before I could down to write. The bed had to be stripped and changed.

The plants had to be watered immediately. When I found myself eying the oven and thinking about cleaning it, I admitted that I was well into procrastination world. I forced myself to sit down in my writing chair, called Diva Dog to join me, took a deep breath, and opened my laptop.

Even though I don't always practice what I preach[174], I do try to be honest with myself. When I work with my students or coaching clients, I encourage them to sit with their feelings of discomfort or unease and ask themselves: what am I really feeling here and why. Both grading and cleaning are activities that I usually take any opportunity to deter a bit longer; therefore, my choosing them over writing, something that I love to do, is a signal that there is something else happening. I also know that I can be stubborn with myself and if I tried to dive right into trying to discern my discomfort it would be a fight. As a distraction I decided to wash my dishes.[175]

---

[171] I think this is another hold over of my impostor syndrome. Maybe it's a byproduct of my reluctance to accept the Creative title. It's probably a bit of both.
[172] Many of the memories I've shared in here are things I forgot even happened
[173] You know you're in serious procrastination mode when grading is your activity of choice instead of the activity being avoided.
[174] I admit how much of an understatement that is.
[175] Unlike the others, this moment of cleaning was not an act of procrastination.

I have a dishwasher that I make good use of, but I will sometimes wash dishes by hand. I find the process of filling the sink with soapy water, immersing the dishes in the water, using the dish rag to wipe or scrub off food detritus, and then rinsing each dish clean to be a meditative process. Above my sink I have a window that looks out over my backyard, and I will stare aimlessly out it as my hands go through the motions of cleaning. On more than one occasion I have been joined in my meditative cleansing with a deer wandering through the bushes and trees behind my house or the local resident groundhog sneaking into the yard to make a snack of plants. It makes sense then that today's dishwashing meditation led me to the realization that I was mourning the loss of this daily writing ritual. When I finally asked myself: what am I really feeling here? The first thing that came to my mind was sadness and loss. I realized that I was grieving the fact that this would be my last day of this writing challenge. The success of completing the challenge by writing every day was overcome by the impending loss of the ritual of the process of this phase of writing.

More than the ritual itself, however, I realized I was also missing my audience. This realization is interesting, since throughout the writing process, the only audience has been me and maybe Diva Dog when she takes a moment to look at my computer screen. The audience I am missing, then, is a hypothetical future collective, not a static group of individuals currently present with me. Despite this fact, I feel a sense of community with them, with you. Every time I have sat down to write, I feel the energy of these others coursing through me. Thinking about these future others coming to these words, interacting with them, meditating on them, creating from them has been the inspiration and motivation to bring me to the keyboard even on those days when fatigue and stress weighed me down. I feel a sense of community with them and have felt embraced with their energy each time I have sat down to write. There is nothing to say that I can't keep writing daily meditations, and perhaps I will.

However, one of the important things that has emerged from these meditations is the importance of not letting yourself get bogged down in your creativity, getting in your own way. I need to allow this project to blossom into its full being, which means shifting from pure writing mode to editing and formatting mode.

As I continue to sit with these feelings of sadness and loss, I am realizing how much these feelings creep into my other creative projects. Throughout these meditations, I have mentioned the various writing projects and paintings I have momentarily abandoned. The first time I thought about writing about these things I paused and wondered if that was a good thing. I felt shame admitting that even though I am writing meditations to help motivate and inspire others to embrace their creativity in any and all forms, I have these unfinished creative projects cluttering my house and my mind. To make this admission I had to accept and embrace the vulnerability inherent within it. I also had to have faith that those individuals who read these words would not judge my inability to complete the projects but instead would find a lesson or inspiration in my talking about them.

Today's dishwashing moment helped me understand yet another facet of why these projects have been temporarily abandoned. As long as they are in process, I don't have to mourn their ending. I get to continue to return to the energy and zeitgeist they generate, even if they create guilt as well. I don't have to say goodbye to them and can continue to live with them. However, as I've discussed in these meditations, that rose colored vision of them is only part of the story. Their continued presence in their abandoned phases also generates feelings of personal shame and incompetence. Perhaps it is time for me not only to get these projects finished, but also to take off my rose colored glasses' way of looking at them.

What both my procrastination to tackle this meditation and my abandoned projects miss is that endings are not the end. How's that for a confusing statement? The ending of a project is the beginning of something new. When I finish a painting I open room for a new painting. I also create the possibility for the energy held in that painting to benefit another person when they hang it on their wall. The circles of energy continue to expand outward benefitting all of us. This is also a good reminder that I need to breathe deep and remind myself that this same thing will happen when I officially leave the academy. I will be ending my college teaching career, and I will be creating the space to expand the ways I teach, allowing myself more time to embrace my creativity.

As I am quickly moving toward the ending of this meditation and this phase of this project, I feel compelled to offer some sort of deep words or thoughts. Maybe, however, that's just the baggage of my years of working in academia telling me I have to always tie things up with a pretty bow and send my students off to their next phases of learning. In higher ed, we have the luxury of living our lives in 15-16 week increments. No matter how bad a semester is, you know there is always an end date to it after which you will take a short break and then begin anew to try again. This schedule makes it easy to tie up those pretty bows. In life outside the academy, however, we have to keep finding ways to push on and move forward.

While I don't have that pretty bow, what I do have are some final words. When times are rough, you have to hope that a change will come soon. Finding a way to be present during these times and let yourself fully glow can be difficult. To do so requires an intentional focus and dedication. For me, embracing creativity is the life source that helps me do this. I know that if I don't take time to create something every day, I will quickly get bogged down in the muck and mire of life. I will succumb to those negative thoughts and get caught on the hamster wheel of worry. I will miss out on the fullness of life by not being present and attuned to the texture and depth of the details of existence. I will continue to get in my own way.

Self, presence, creativity. These things don't end. They continue. I continue. This ending is my beginning.

I Am a Renaissance Man

The journey of writing this manuscript has taken me in directions I never anticipated. I have dusted off memories that have been sitting in storage for years, sometimes decades. I have explored creative avenues I didn't even know were of potential interest. Perhaps most surprisingly, however, is how many different ways and times I found myself getting out of my way and forcing myself to keep moving forward. The fact that you're reading this now means I was able to find enough self-compassion and get out of my own way.

When I first challenged myself to write for 30 days on whatever messages arose, I vaguely thought I would write a book. I don't think I ever actually thought I would follow through with publishing that book. Writing is fun and exciting; editing is tedious and hard work. No matter how often I help others transform their nascent writings into publishable works, I'm not always good at following my own advice. As became clear to me in thinking about my connections to my own creativity, I realized I have a hard time letting my creations go. They become like little written friends who provide me solace and comfort in knowing they are sitting there on my table or desk simply waiting for me to return to them. Once I accepted this, I challenged myself[176] to get out of my own way and let this piece of creativity be different.

Notwithstanding my love of a challenge and my desire to never let myself down, there were many points along the way where I found

---

[176] Again with the personal challenges. I'm pretty sure I get this competitive streak from my grandfather.

reasons to pause. I first started editing in winter and then paused when my teaching schedule became too much. I returned to editing in spring and then paused when spring yard work called to me. I tried again in early summer and then paused when it was time for family vacation. What I find especially interesting about all of these attempted starts is that despite putting the manuscript on the backburner, it kept calling to me. I like to think that in addition to being infused with my story and energies, it is also blessed with the energies of my friends and ancestors whose stories are peppered throughout. The interweaving of these energies provided the push I needed to keep returning to these pages and move them forward.

Once I finally decided to edit for real, I made it a point to touch the pages every day. I like to edit on hard copy, so I had actual pieces of paper to touch. Somedays I only managed to pull the pages out and glance over them. Other days, I found myself joyfully immersed in the editing process. I would grab my binder of pages needing to be edited and my purple pen[177], I would pour a cup of coffee, and move to the loveseat in my studio. Diva Dog would hop up next to me for a quick pet and then jump onto the top of the love seat where she can keep a close guard on me by barking at anyone who dares to walk down the street. The process quickly became a ritual[178] that I looked forward to and that helped me stay focused on working my way through editing. On most days, I would edit for an hour or so and then take a break to work on whatever canvas was in progress. After painting I would spend some time reading. In the spring I decided to deep dive into cognitive processing and the placebo

---

[177] While I love the color purple, there was no significance to the choice of this pen in the beginning. It was merely the one that was closest to where I first sat to work. After a couple days, however, I decided the edits had to all be done in purple.

[178] I clearly love rituals as much as I love challenges.

effect. While I am familiar with a lot of the spiritual stuff in this area, wanted to specifically to read and learn the science aspects as well.[179]

During this time, I realized that I was finally living out my childhood dreams of being a Renaissance Man. I was doing a lot of different things in a lot of different areas and doing them well. [180] I was writing. I was painting. I was teaching. I was studying. I was advocating. I was baking. I found myself happily living in the jack of all trades world. I even embraced the Artist title that I struggled with during the initial writing of this. I came home one day to find the new bookcase I had ordered sitting outside my front door. The box was nearly seven feet long and weighed close to 100 pounds. While struggling to find a way to push/shove it into the house, a pair of painters driving by stopped to help me.[181] They easily moved the box into my studio and noticed my paintings in process. One of them paused in front of the easel and said, "Wow, you're an artist. I love this." Without hesitation I said, "Yes, I am. Thank you."

It would seem, then, that I had finally mastered the art of self-compassion and successfully getting out of my own way. You would think. When I first started thinking about publishing this I had a few potential publishers in mind. One day while randomly scrolling on social media, I saw a post from one of them, Tehom Publishing. I read the post as an act of synchronicity and decided to message with a query before I had time to overthink it. The response came quickly[182] and was positive. I found myself excited and newly energized in my quests to edit my raw ramblings into something

---

[179] It became a running joke with my friends to ask me if I planned to return to school for yet another degree in neuro-science. I can't say that the thought never crossed my mind.
[180] I'm still waiting to master the four hours of sleep trick, however.
[181] In my surprised gratitude I neglected to get their names.
[182] After a professional lifetime of dealing with academic publishing where response times can take weeks and months, anything else seems especially decadent.

readable. Within a few hours, though, Peggy's voice wormed its way to the top of my thoughts with questions: "Are you sure publishing this is a good idea?"; "Why don't you wait until you've had more time to work on this?"; Does anyone really want to read your ramblings?"

I fell into a recursive pattern. I would move the process forward by sending in a formal proposal, getting positive feedback, feel elated for a few hours quickly followed by Peggy's questions. Each step along the way from sending in samples, to agreeing on a publication date, to signing the publishing contract followed this pattern. In the past, I'm pretty sure I would have succumbed to the fears hiding behind Peggy's questions and added this manuscript to my other abandoned works in progress. This time, however, I lived into the reality of embracing my creativity and the fears that accompany it. I thanked Peggy for her concerns and clicked send, officially starting the publication process.

I share all this because it's an important reminder that mastering self-compassion isn't a one-shot deal. It's a continual back and forth negotiation. It's a journey whose end point keeps getting pushed just a bit further out. The good thing, however, is that each step forward is progress. It's movement toward acceptance. It's something I will continue to work on mastering and talking about with anyone who will listen.[183]

---

[183] In the spirit of honesty, I'll be talking it about even with those who won't or don't want to listen.

Tehom Center Publishing

Tehom Center Publishing is a non-profit imprint publishing feminist and queer authors, with a particular commitment to elevate BIPOC authors. In addition to traditional, independent publishing, Tehom Center Publishing offers individual and group coaching programs aimed at empowering authors in their book writing, book marketing, and book entrepreneurship. Learn more at www.tehomcenter.org

www.ingramcontent.com/pod-product-compliance
Lightning Source LLC
Chambersburg PA
CBHW071326120626
46546CB00002B/465